The 8-Day Week

The 8-Day Week

John Ward Pearson

HARPER & ROW, PUBLISHERS

New York, Evanston, San Francisco, London

1817

Designed by Sidney Feinberg

For Alfred William Lever, Ph.D., deceased. In
seven years of teaching, Al brought more human
understanding to those he encountered than most
of us can in an average lifetime. This book
is an attempt to add to his work.

Contents

Acknowledgments

The basic concept of dividing the country's labor force into two groups, who would work in alternating 4-day cycles, was suggested by Richard P. Urfer. Without that concept, and his continued moral and financial support during the eighteen months it took to develop and express a workable version of that idea, this book would not exist.

Others deserving deepest thanks include Ellen Chaput, who somehow found the time and energy to type and retype this book; Hugh Van Dusen, of Harper & Row, who not only committed his firm to an untried author but also devoted a great deal of his own patience and skill to somehow elicit a usable manuscript from what began as a literary shambles; and Lars Sjöwall, who generously lent me a little house in Sweden where I could start wrestling with the double problem of imagining the structure and consequences of an original concept on the one hand and finding ways to describe it on the other.

Special thanks are extended to Roy and Sylvia Carter for their generous English hospitality as the writing progressed, and to Mike Beldock, Roger Bumstead, Marty Karlin, Jack Taylor, and many, many others who contributed relevant material and moral support.

Thanks to you all, dear friends.

Introduction:
What This Book Is About

On the surface, this book offers an alternative means of arranging our work and leisure time to help us cope with the strains commonly associated with modern urban life, while creating the opportunity to relax and have fun.

The subject, however, becomes more complex than this as various implications of the 8-Day Week are explored. In fact, the subject becomes the total of all our lives as we presently live them, and how we might get more out of them if given the opportunity. As a result, such diverse matters as education, health, urban renewal, psychology, marriage and divorce, taxes, economics, sports, and gerontology come under discussion, making this a handbook for living as much as anything else. Frankly, nobody is equipped to write learnedly on such a tremendous variety of topics. Still, I have done my best in the belief that a start toward a better life must be made somewhere—that once interest has been sparked and hope rekindled among a broad segment of the population, the energies and expertise of many may join to achieve the kind of better life the 8-Day Week promises us all.

The 8-Day Week

1 ■ A Brief Survey of Our Urban Ills
■

Headaches; Traffic Jams; Pollution;
Stagnant Productivity; Unemployment

Things are not going well for urban dwellers. Since over two-thirds of this country's entire population lives in urban areas, it could further be said that things are not going well in the United States. The things that are not going well can be grouped under two broad headings: the quality of our lives, which is suffering from apparently insoluble urban congestion, and economic difficulties—specifically, unemployment and inflation born of an imbalance between costs and increases in productivity.

This book carries a suggestion as to how these quietly disastrous social and economic trends can be reversed, while arresting the ominous direction that taxes continue to take. It also suggests that in the process of following the recommendations it contains, we will be given our lives back, to live as we like.

Before entering into these proposals, however, a review of a variety of situations and portents surrounding us daily is felt to be in order. The remainder of this chapter is devoted to such stage setting and highlighting.

We have become so accustomed to deterioration in the quality of city life that we can somehow find amusement in a show called *The Prisoner of Second Avenue*, a play, according to the *New York Times*, "about a man who is beset by urban despairs." When looked at coolly, a play about urban people's despairs doesn't sound very funny. Neither does a phenomenon called "the urban headache," which has been described in *New York* magazine as being a "symptom of a harried organism." A long article on the subject carried all the grisly details. It estimated that in New York, headaches took third place in commonly occurring physical activity, behind sex and eating. The point was made that as city size increases, intensity of headaches increases. On a parallel, it was noted proudly that though other cities have doctors and doctors' associations specializing in headache, only New York City possesses a full-time headache clinic. It is only to be expected that the clinic has a four-month waiting list. *New York* listed several reasons for epidemic headaches: inhalation of toxic fumes while trapped in 10,000-car traffic jams; tension; emotional strain; aggravation born of "inscrutable telephone systems, inoperable trains, intolerable subways."

It is pitiful that a major magazine, oriented to city life, finds itself being truly useful by delving into urban headaches. It is equally pitiful that five of the ten recommended courses of action to be taken in case of urban headache treat *symptoms* rather than *causes*; that two preventive measures (exercise and rest) are beyond the reach of the majority, while two more require a major psychological adjustment (frustration/perfectionism), and the remaining directive requires one to eat at his desk or in a meeting. Perhaps it's all part of life as constituted for city dwellers in a highly capitalized society such as America's.

Not that we can take any comfort in the fact, but we are not alone in our problem of urban headaches or at least one of their causes. The following excerpts from the *Wall Street Journal* would lead us to believe we are among the luckiest people (still) alive:

The international Road Federation recently calculated the number of motor vehicles per mile of road in major nations. Top of the list: Britain, with 62.5 vehicles per mile. Numbers two through seven were other West European nations. Number eight: The U.S., with 28.6 vehicles per mile.

"You see what is happening," says Antonio Addamiano, chief of the motor vehicle department in the Italian Transport Ministry. "It is chaos." . . .

Britain's 1,000th mile of motorway isn't due for completion until next year. However, Peter Walker, government secretary for the environment, recently outlined a program designed to create a "comprehensive network" by the 1980's, at a cost of several billion dollars.

Italy also has motorway problems. Emanuele Scotto, chief engineer for the national highway authority, says that since 1960 the ratio of road mileage to autos has dropped by 56%.

"There are too many cars and too few roads," he says.

Only a confirmed urban masochist can find joy in the fact that Britain has more than twice as many vehicles per mile of road than the U.S. He is also forgetting that the uncountable miles of uncrowded farm roads, highways, and superhighways which crisscross relatively lightly populated rural expanses of our larger country are part of the dividend in calculating miles of road per vehicle and play no part in easing urban traffic problems.

In a letter to Mayor Lindsay, one-time New York City Air Resources Commissioner Robert N. Rickles is quoted by the *New York Times* as having averred that "The total chaos of auto traffic and trucking . . . is slowly but surely strangling the economic viability of the midtown area as well as polluting the air." He also alluded in the same letter to saving 1.4 million jobs in that part of New York City by rectifying this chaotic traffic situation.

Greater New York, though the largest of our metropolitan areas, has certain characteristics in common with other major cities throughout the country. Among these is a stabilized central city population, accompanied by increasing numbers of suburban and exurban residents.

In recent years, New York City's air grew increasingly dirty. Federal law will require an average presence of 75 micrograms or less of suspended particulates per cubic meter of air by 1975.

According to the *New York Times*, New York's progress toward that goal reads as follows for a three-year period:

Particulates per Cubic Meter of New York City Air (Recommended by 1975: 75 micrograms)

1968–69	96.2 micrograms
1969–70	104.8
1970–71	106.5

New York is not alone in its clean-air problems. The Environmental Protection Agency has warned Philadelphia, Washington, D.C., Chicago, Denver, and Los Angeles that they "will have to change their commuting patterns substantially in order to comply with the new [air] standards," according to *U.S. News & World Report*.

The effect of heavy commuter traffic is not limited to air pollution alone. General Electric claims a $2 million yearly loss at a single factory in Philadelphia due to employee lateness caused by traffic congestion, and the Southern California Plan Association has estimated that unless something is done to prevent it, traffic in downtown Los Angeles will completely stagnate by 1977.

Between 1945 and 1971, the number of registered motor vehicles nationwide increased by 81 million, from 31 to 112 million, according to *U.S. News & World Report*. At the same time, the number of people using public transit annually declined from 19 billion to roughly 5½ billion. The mission of government at all levels appears to be to force a reversal of these facts. Although mass transit offers many theoretical benefits in terms of reduced traffic congestion and pollution, it also appears to hold certain *real* negatives in the minds of the masses who have rejected it. Governments appear to be more interested, therefore, in forcing a situation through various repressive measures than in relating to a "given" through use of imagination.

Past experience may have taught the battle-weary commuter to distrust promises made on behalf of "improved" public transit systems. He may feel that once mass transportation systems have been erected or revamped, at great cost to him, they will immediately begin to show deterioration in physical terms and quality of service and continually raise fares charged to a now captive market. And he may be right. According to *Business Week*, mass-transit labor costs increased 25 percent over a recent two-year period and now amount to two-thirds of total operating costs. The general manager of the Cleveland Transit System was quoted by *Business Week* as having said, "Transit has practically no way of improving worker productivity. We can't develop a bigger machine like manufacturers. We are stopped right on the surface street where we operate."

This man is not the only one who is being frustrated by lack of increases in productivity from his men and machines in combination. Even industries which *can* build bigger machines have encountered problems in productivity, using the loosest possible definition of "productivity": output per man-hour. The Bureau of Labor Statistics indicates that in 1970, for example, output per man-hour declined in fifteen of thirty-nine industries surveyed, compared with 1969 levels. Two examples of labor productivity (which is only one of many elements which should be considered in calculating an operation's productivity) in two capital-intensive industries are shown in the graphs on pages 6 and 7. The widening gaps between output and hourly wage trends can be roughly characterized as inflation.

These graphs do not really reflect the situation in which we as workers find ourselves, because they are confined to manufacturing situations. Most of us, on the other hand, are employed in service industries, in which it is frequently even harder to "build bigger machines," if any machines existed in the first place. In fact, approximately two-thirds of working men and women are involved in the provision of services. In commenting on the dilemma posed by attempts to increase service-related productivity, *Time* magazine had this, in part, to say:

. . . a mere .1% increase in productivity this year would add $1 billion to the gross national product. . . .

Indexes of Output/Production Man-Hour:
Steel Industry
Versus
Indexes of Average Hourly Earnings:
Primary Metals Industries

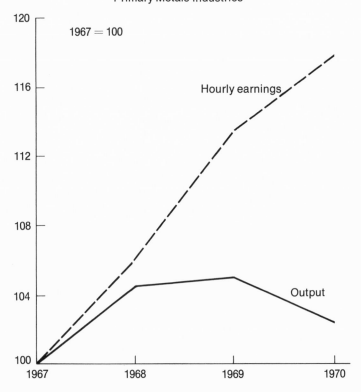

Yet, there are important factors working against any productivity surge. Not least are deep-rooted difficulties in improving output per man-hour in many service fields. Increasing the number of a doctor's patients or the size of a teacher's class could be taken as improving their "productivity," but the dilution of quality in the services they perform would probably be unacceptable. . . .

Says Robert Nathan, a member of Time's Board of Economists: "We need a hell of a big push on the economy through increased Government spending. This would lead to greater demand, lower unemploy-

Indexes of Output/Production Man-Hour

Versus

Indexes of Average Hourly Earnings:

Motor Vehicles and Equipment

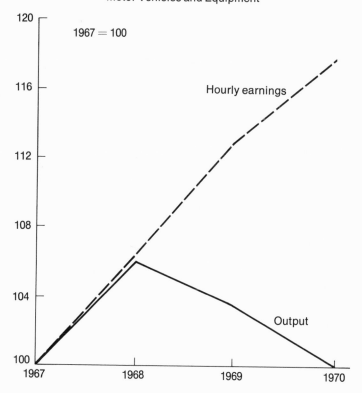

ment, higher plant utilization and productivity, and give us a better chance to fight inflation." That is the reverse of traditional economic dogma, which holds that a rapid business expansion creates the danger of feeding inflation—but traditional economic dogmas do not seem to be working any more.

It is difficult to disagree with the allegation that traditional economic dogmas do not seem to be working, but I frankly doubt that massive government spending represents either any kind of departure from our present and past economic course or a solution to present problems. Government already accounts for over one-third of total gross national product. We have, over a period of years, had a succession of pump-priming activities take the form of direct and indirect public spending; for example: WPA, PWA, TVA, WWII, Korea, NASA, urban renewal programs, FHA, Vietnam, accelerated depreciation schedules, and investment tax credits. Our present situation is where all this has got us. The notion of gigantic increases in government spending carries with it the specter of proportionate increases in taxes, greater public debt, and more dollars spent to pay off such debts with interest. Such an approach does not seem particularly imaginative. On the other hand, it might tend to keep inflation spiraling alongside taxes. Such a situation would tend to create more ill effects of the kind to which we have become unhappily accustomed, ultimately including even higher levels of persistent unemployment—the last item scheduled for discussion as a background signpost of what the present holds and the future promises for the 1970s.

The Bureau of Labor Statistics indicates that between 1950 and 1970, almost 20 million people were added to the work force, the totals going from 58,920,000 to 78,627,000, for an over-all increase of 33 percent. Within this total, male employment rose 18 percent, from 41,580,000 to 48,960,000, and female employment from 17,340,000 to 29,667,000—a 71 percent increase.

The total numbers of the unemployed also increased between 1950 and 1970, from 3,288,000 to 4,088,000—a 24 percent increase.

Since then, the situation has deteriorated somewhat and stabilized. The recovery of the economy in 1972 failed to materially reduce the percentage levels of unemployment, which tend to be officially reported as being roughly 5 to 5½ percent of the country's available labor force. This failure is substantially traceable to large increases in the number of people entering the labor market, which cannot be assimilated by more slowly expanding labor demand. There are, in addition, experts who dispute the unemployment levels reported by the Bureau of Labor Statistics. The following excerpts from a major article in the *New York Post* offer a fair idea of the scope of such unofficial estimates and the extent of their disagreement with official statistics regarding unemployment levels:

"We say there are around nine million people unemployed today . . ." says David Livingston, president of the 30,000-member union of wholesale, retail, office and shipping workers in this city. . . .

Several factors are cited by Bertram Gross, professor of urban affairs at Hunter College. . . .

"A lot of people drop out of the labor force and are not counted, even though they might like a job. They are the people who became discouraged and are too smart to continue looking for jobs that aren't there," says Gross, who served as executive secretary to the Council of Economic Advisers between 1946 and 1952.

Then, there is a large category of employables, mostly recent students, who have never worked. They do not register as jobless and they are not included in the Government's unemployment figures.

A third group the statistics do not reveal are those working part-time who would prefer full-time jobs, according to Gross.

A fourth group consists of those working below their abilities, he said.

If the people in these four categories were counted, Gross estimates that unemployment could be considered to be nine million or more.

Depending on who is doing the estimating, and on what basis, domestic unemployment levels are either discouraging or very discouraging. High levels of unemployment have certain unfortunate effects on the health of an economy or several interlocking economies. Large numbers of unemployed individuals not only represent direct costs in the form of various types of public support but also create what has been termed a GNP gap, which can be described as the difference between what is actually being achieved and what *could be* achieved if the situation were different. The effect of this latter consideration is not limited merely to the country's own economy. Other countries' economies are also dependent, to varying degrees, on the health of the United States, the world's largest importer.

The expenditure of enormous sums of government money, in addition to what has been and is being spent, represents no solution to the country's basic problems, which are, in turn, essentially urban. City life will continue to make us physically unhealthy as well as neurotic. The air will stay dirty; we will continue to have unemployment and inflation; huge capital investments along accustomed lines will probably fail to solve problems in the area of productivity.

Some of the fruits of past and current efforts to solve our problems in the same old way are briefly catalogued in the following chapter. In the same vein, certain concepts which have been taught to and accepted generally by society are reexamined with results which can be fairly described as interesting.

2   We're Getting Less for More

■

Transportation Problems; Overloaded Switchboards;
Slowly Rising Incomes; Rapidly Rising Taxes;
The Need for a New Approach; The 8-Day Week

What we are getting in our lives is less for more. The process of earning and spending more and more dollars to achieve increasingly less meaningful results is a disheartening one to encounter for those who have been brought up expecting to attain the reverse. The dollar, along with the technology it spawns and supports, is becoming increasingly impotent to solve our mundane daily problems. The void created by money's growing inability to provide answers is being filled by the modern equivalent of coolie labor, i.e., individuals' putting up with, or learning to circumvent, obstacles to the average city dweller's leading a relatively unfettered existence. Several examples of both the frustrations and our failure to buy our way out of urban living problems follow.

One of the most obvious urban problems is transportation. Although the largest inner cities have reached plateaus in terms of population levels, suburban and exurban populations have grown rapidly. *U.S. News & World Report* estimates that suburban populations increased by 26 percent between 1960 and 1970. Although some of these growing suburbs are self-contained in the sense of domiciling commerce as well as families, many are purely bedroom communities, where working men and women spend their nights but not their days. Their days involve commuting to and from the central cities where they work. The travel facilities available to carry this flood of commuters are commonly inadequate to meet the needs they are supposed to accommodate.

Commuter railroads are a joke. Around New York, for instance, fares are constantly being raised for users of the Penn Central, Jersey Central, and Long Island railroads. When fares are not being raised, hearings seem always to be taking place *about* further fare increases. A regular commuter on any of these lines will assure you that these fare increases do not reflect the cost of improved service. To the contrary, equipment tends to be decrepit, schedules are systematically pared, and timetables show a tendency toward being more editorial than factual.

New York's subway service is frequently and endlessly criticized. Subway fares, on the other hand, have increased 600 percent, from a nickel to 35 cents, since 1950.

Bridge and tunnel tolls around Manhattan have doubled, presumably to help pay the increased cost of providing mass transportation, which used to be cheap but is becoming less so, and to discourage private cars from entering the city—thus reducing traffic jams and air pollution while encouraging motorists to use already inadequate commuting facilities. Perhaps a more constructive and intelligent attitude toward problems of congestion and their solution can be found in the handling of the Oakland Bay Bridge, which offers toll-free crossing to car pools and bills bus lines monthly.

This approach at least makes a positive effort to improve the commuter's lot. It also offers some incentive, in the form of toll-free passage, to encourage motorists to follow a socially productive course (pooling) if their circumstances permit, rather than categorically handicapping those who commute by car, as is the case in Manhattan. Helpful and positive as the Bay area's approach may be, on the other hand it is doubtful that this tack represents anything resembling a true solution to San Francisco–Oakland's traffic difficulties.

The transportation problem there, in New York, and in virtually all urban areas around the country is twofold: first, existing facilities are inadequate to meet peak demand, which occurs mornings and evenings, Mondays through Fridays, when people attempt to go to and from work, and second, the cost of expanding these facilities is simply huge. *Business Week* quotes Transportation Undersecretary James Beggs as estimating the cost of *already existing* roads at $500 billion. That figure, of course, is heavily weighted by older, cheaper roads—built before the specter of present-day road construction costs presented itself. An example of today's costs can be found in a cloverleaf recently constructed in the Bronx. The price: $68 million.

The federal government estimates that 20,900,000 acres of the United States are devoted to roads and roadway. To that we are adding new concrete at the rate of 75,000 miles of new roadway per year.

Despite these awesome statistics, it is tough, and getting tougher, to go to and from work. The facilities are there: the freeways, throughways, tollways, parkways, expressways, beltways, highways, and one-ways. But they are insufficient to meet the challenge of peak-load demand. They are systematically overtaxed at predictable, regimented times on certain selected days of the week. During other, also predictable days of the week, these same arteries are drastically underused. Such a situation represents bad management of available assets.

Having apparently been stymied in their attempts to resolve traffic problems by one means or another, civic leaders and federal transportation experts are turning to mass transit, particularly rapid transit, as the hoped-for solution. At least twelve U.S. cities are now in various stages of planning, financing, or constructing rapid-transit systems in the hope that these cities' strangulation will thereby be averted. Included among these are San Francisco's, at a cost of $1.5 billion, Washington, D.C.'s, at $3.1 billion, and a newly proposed system for Los Angeles at an *estimated* ultimate cost of $3 to $6 billion. Mass-transit systems are expensive, as can be seen from these lines on the subject taken from *Business Week:*

The kind of money Beggs is talking about turned up in a study done for the Urban Mass Transportation Administration (UMTA), showing it would cost less than $40-billion to upgrade and expand city transit systems in this decade. William J. Ronan, head of New York State's powerful Metropolitan Transit Authority (MTA), argues that if this money can "provide the kind of transit system the public needs, we're not talking in terms the federal government can't afford."

Perhaps $40 billion spent over ten years on mass transit doesn't sound extravagant when viewed in terms of a federal budget, but it looks somewhat more expensive when viewed with the realization that federal budgets equal *taxpayers' money*. As to whether the subject $40 billion in sum, or its parts, really promises the hoped-for panacea, perhaps the following excerpts from a *New York Times* article are useful:

"The problem," one Transportation Department official said when asked about the argument, "is that rapid transit has become too much like motherhood. You can't discuss it rationally, at least in public." . . .

One opponent, George Hilton, an economics professor who specializes in transportation at the University of California at Los Angeles, calls the project "a fiasco." "There is just no market for it," he asserted.

Mr. Hilton, who was also critical of plans of Atlanta, Baltimore and other cities to build rail systems, said: "What they're doing is making a huge investment in a declining market. Every place you look, the number of trips into the central business district is the most rapidly declining segment of urban transportation."

Former Transportation Secretary Volpe is quoted by *Business Week* as being "convinced that technology will produce more efficient transportation with a high pay-off on a relatively small dollar investment." Other experts, including at least one of Mr. Volpe's own employees, seem less convinced. Robert H. Cannon, Jr., Assistant Transportation Secretary for systems development

—i.e., the head technocrat—is also quoted by *Business Week*, as saying, "Transportation needs an infusion of technology, but we've got to handle the more mundane problems first."

Urban dwellers who must travel to and from work are highly familiar with these mundane problems.

We have come increasingly to rely on the telephone as a basic means of communication. We have also come increasingly to distrust the telephone as a basic means of communication. This picture tends to be rounded out somewhat more by the following words from the *New York Times:*

The Public Service Commission today approved a $160 million increase in telephone rates, averaging about 9 per cent more statewide for the consumer.

Calling the increase "distressingly large," the commission sought to soften it by ordering the New York Telephone Company to pay $1.50 monthly rebates to a minority of customers with the worst phone service. The commission described the rebate order as "historic."

The increase . . . follows a "temporary" $190 million rate rise last summer. . . . The effect of the two rises, which total $350-million, will be to lift the phone rates for most New York City users 29 per cent above what they were before last July 9. . . .

"Of major concern is the possibility that telephone service will be priced out of the reach of the less-affluent members of society," the commission's 108-page decision declared.

"The major culprit" in rising costs is the phone company's "rapidly expanding capital plant," the commission declared. . . .

The commission also authorized increases in the company's charge for installations, roughly doubling the current costs, to $12.50 for a residence and $25 for a business.

The "culprit"—the rapidly expanding capital plant—exists because of the need to meet a tremendous surge of telephoning during predictable hours (9–5) on certain days of the week (Monday–Friday). In fact, AT&T's capital needs are virtually insatiable. According to *Time,* Ma Bell will invest $8.5 billion in new capital during 1973 alone. This sum represents approximately one-tenth of *all new private investment* projected for that year. Such tremendous demand for money at one source has the less obvious effect of making money somewhat scarce—that is, more expensive in terms of interest charged to individuals who borrow money to finance a home or pay a hospital bill. It is clear, then, that over-strained facilities, on the one hand, and great pressure on the capital market to fill the facilities gap, on the other, are com-bining to give us less communication for more money. If we could discover a means of better managing our communications needs, service would improve, the necessity for capital expansion in telephone systems would be reduced sharply, and when further ex-pansion needs did occur, they would tend to do so more gradually, thus causing less dislocation and less overtime—two types of costs which we, the consumers, will also pay.

The example given in Chapter 1 of New York's getting dirtier despite increased efforts to the contrary on the city's part is one illustration of less for more. Another illustration of less for more can be seen in these excerpts from a *New York Times* article regarding a sewage disposal plant:

> The vast sewage-treatment plant that the city wants to build on Harlem's Hudson River shore will cost $751.9-million—twice as much as last year's estimated cost—the City Planning Commission was told yesterday.
> "This is an incredible increase," Commissioner Martin Gallant pro-tested as the planner heard the capital budget requests for the En-vironmental Protection Administration. . . .
> In 1967, when the project was first being discussed, its cost was estimated at $70-million. . . .
> Mr. Lang said . . . the foundation work, estimated by the con-sultants at $100-million, was *bid* at $229-million. . . .

No one would argue against the advisability of treating a major city's sewage, but it is interesting to note that between 1967 and early 1972, the estimated cost rose *by more than ten times,* from

$70 million to $751.9 million. Regardless of how this project is funded, the money to pay for it will come from the taxpayers—very few of whom have managed a 1,000 percent raise in any four-year period.

I think we suffer from a pair of illusions: (1) that over a period of many years, average personal *real* incomes have grown tremendously; (2) that over the past decade (between 1960 and 1970), *real* incomes have not grown at a normal rate due to pernicious inflation.

U.S. Department of Commerce figures show that, in fact, our average per capita disposable *real* incomes, adjusted to reflect losses in purchasing power, have increased 109 percent in the forty-one years between 1929 and 1970. That averages out to 2.65 percent per year over the entire period. At this rate of change, if you are single and earn $10,000 *constant* dollars this year, and show average progress, next year you can expect to earn $10,265 *constant* dollars . . . and, after forty-one years, you will have managed to work your way up to a peak of $20,900 *constant* dollars. It was a slow haul between 1929 and 1970.

The last decade, on the other hand, has been an outstanding one in terms of increasing per capita *real* incomes. The yearly average growth between 1960 and 1970 was nearly 3.8 percent. Using that growth factor along with the earlier $10,000 constant-dollar income example means that next year you'd be earning $10,380, which feels about the same as $10,265.

The point of the above is, *most of us are not going to become rich in terms of money over the course of our working lives.* If you accept that point, stop to consider for a moment how hard you are working to achieve your nongoal of becoming nonrich. Furthermore, consider the fact that it is becoming harder to work, not easier. Harder in terms of meeting increased job complexity, harder in terms of educational or training requirements, harder in terms of the need to make more decisions faster. It's even harder (as has been pointed out) to get to and from work.

The fact that most of us are *not* working to get rich holds important implications in terms of our goals and our lives, because the act of achieving our goals is the act of living out our lives.

Taxes generate the revenue used by various government agencies to pay for the maintenance or improvement of our living standards. During the decade 1960–70, state and local per capita taxes more than doubled. Yearly state and local tax payments *per person* now exceed $500 in Hawaii, Washington, D.C., Wisconsin, Connecticut, New York, Massachusetts, Michigan, California, and Maryland, according to the *New York Times.*

These increases help to dramatize further the *less for more* syndrome, particularly when contrasted to the deterioration in the quality of our urban lives.

The most meaningful part of our lives occurs between the ages of twenty and sixty. During that span, we leave our parents' homes and form our own households, marry and have our own children, and attain our own identities, both in terms of self and as they relate to our social and economic situation. This is the interval in which the greater portion of our lives actually occurs—arithmetically in terms of the number of days this period contains, and qualitatively in terms of the experiences we encounter: the happiness, fulfillment, or whatever else we find before we die.

These years, during which potential life satisfaction is to be either realized or lost forever, are also the years during which we work for a living. And it is here where we are taking the worst beating of all when it comes to getting less for more. Our lives are being trammeled increasingly by forces which are beyond our control. Our prime years are becoming less and less rewarding in human terms as we allocate ever greater quantities of time and effort in the attempt to cope with contemporary urban life.

Some of the elements which go into making urban life increasingly unpleasant and unlivable have been cast up previously.

No mention has yet been made, however, of the basic causes which are responsible for making what should be the best years of our lives fail to achieve their potential. Our lives are being mismanaged by:

- CUSTOM
- HABIT
- THOUGHTLESSNESS

CUSTOM—It is customary for us to work for a living certain days of the week—Monday through Friday—and to delegate the remaining days to other activities, officially if not actually leisure oriented. We put in an official 40-hour week which, according to the Bureau of Labor Statistics, actually contains 37 hours' working time. We all go to work together. We all work together. We all come home together. We also take our weekends together, straining in unison to do our weekend chores or to seek relief from our daily working lives—again, in competition with everyone else—because that is the custom. This custom is costing us all, with the exception perhaps of the very rich, a great deal of valuable time.

HABIT—Because it is the custom to work for a living Mondays through Fridays, and to reserve Saturdays and Sundays for other activities, we have acquired the habit of going through the mill with everyone else. We have been conditioned, as individuals, to expect this situation. We have come to expect the things that are part of the normal workday and weekend situations—the crowding, the traffic jams, the delays, the waste of time and energy, the nerves, headache, and hassling to which we have become habituated.

We are not to be blamed for acquiring this social habit. We have been completely conditioned from earliest childhood to the notion that we do certain things at certain times on certain days. We, who have learned and come to accept this habit, are each making a major contribution to the continued mismanagement of our lives, despite the fact that we tend to victimize ourselves by doing so.

THOUGHTLESSNESS—Sufficient consideration has not been given to alternative ways of scheduling our time in terms of earning a living on the one hand, and leading a rewarding private life on the other. Some attempt has been made to conceive and propose alternative ways of organizing our time. Chief among these is the 4-day 40-hour week, with a 3-day weekend. Other approaches include alternating a 7-day workweek with seven days off and split shifts, and staggered working hours, which is designed to lessen pressure on transportation facilities during workdays. Although each of these approaches has something to be said for it, all have serious drawbacks which ultimately make their widespread acceptance and application highly unlikely if not completely out of the question. The advantages and disadvantages of these will be discussed, and their shortcomings made clear, later in the book. In the meantime, let it suffice to state that these approaches do not represent the best alternatives to the 5-day 40-hour week, a working custom which is well past its time.

Based on the above, one might presume that there is no alternative to the 5-day week. But there is. There is a system which is economically viable—which will, in fact, stimulate economic growth and yield increases in worker productivity, which will make it far easier and more pleasant for us to do our work—while at the same time will give us a tremendous opportunity to lead rich personal lives. This system calls for the following:

First, let us *revise the workweek* so that businesses and related activities may remain open and going

- TEN HOURS PER DAY
- SEVEN DAYS PER WEEK

Second, let us *divide the work force* so that, on any given day,

- ONE-HALF OF THE PEOPLE ARE WORKING
- ONE-HALF OF THE PEOPLE ARE OFF

Third, let us *restructure the relationship between our periods of work and our leisure time,* so that each person

- WORKS FOR FOUR DAYS
       AND
- TAKES THE NEXT FOUR DAYS OFF

Fourth, to avert catastrophic traffic jams and *to maintain a smoothly functioning business mechanism,* let workers' "on" and "off" periods be staggered evenly throughout 8-day cycles so that *each day*

- ONE-EIGHTH OF WORKING PEOPLE RETURN TO WORK
       WHILE
- ONE-EIGHTH OF US BEGIN A REST CYCLE

This system is called the 8-Day Week. Subsequent reference to this system will use this term as well as "The Alternative."

The remainder of this book is devoted to discussing the ramifications of the 8-Day Week as it applies to our work, our personal lives, schooling, and the younger generation, problems which will be encountered in adopting this system, along with recommended solutions to these problems, discussion of other possible systems and their shortcomings, how the system is economically justified and how it can be brought into being. Generally, it will be compared to the 5-day 40-hour workweek, because that is the system within which most of us currently operate.

3 Getting the Job Done

■

The New 35-Hour Week Versus No Progress Toward It;
Application to Various Job Situations; Upper
Management; How to Save 15 Extra Days a Year;
Better Skills, Better Jobs, More Money,
(or) More Satisfaction

The idea of reorganizing the business week and related working schedules for individuals to give them half the year off probably holds considerable appeal and intrigue for the average person. Appealing as the notion may be, however, it can have no value unless millions of jobs, entailing a very wide variety of activities, can continue to be performed within the context of such a substantially rearranged system. This chapter is devoted to describing how several types of differing functions might be performed. It also discusses certain benefits accruing to working men and women which might not immediately come to the reader's mind, along with a brief on the progress of leisure, over many years, for working people in this country.

Perhaps the best way to start would be to explain the effect the 8-Day Week would have on the "workweek" as we currently know it.

The Alternative calls for our working four 10-hour days out of every eight, rather than five 8-hour days out of every seven. To compute the average "weekly" hours worked, take this system to a yearly basis, then divide by 52 to obtain a weekly average—leaving out vacation time, lunch hours, coffee breaks, and holidays, which are variables—as follows:

1. 4 workdays out of every 8 = 182.5 workdays per year;
2. 182.5 workdays × 10 hours per day = 1,825 work hours per year;
3. 1,825 ÷ 52 = *35 hours per week.*

The system, then, represents a 35-hour week *before* lunch and coffee breaks. Compared to the present 5-day 40-hour week, the 8-Day Week offers a 12½ percent reduction in actual weekly work hours. This stated saving in work time is valid and accurate. Those who do not believe the majority of us work a 40-hour week should be aware of Bureau of Labor Statistics data on the subject. In 1970, for example, total nonagricultural private employees worked 37 hours and 12 minutes per week on the average. To that *must be added* time for lunch and coffee breaks, if any. The addition of five half-hour lunches brings the weekly total to roughly 39 hours; one 10-minue coffee break per day brings the total close to 40 hours, and two such coffee breaks brings the weekly total to *more than* 40 hours.

In other words, the 8-Day Week offers the first substantial reduction in average weekly work time in over thirty years. In fact the concept of leisure time, and its accession to becoming a real part of a working person's natural existence, did not gain much currency until the 1920s. During earliest settlement days, the work of clearing and maintaining farmland carried with it the consuming need to devote virtually full time to the tasks at hand. Farmers were accustomed to working from dawn to dusk 6 days per week. The idea of doing "a day's work" persisted in the industrial era, despite the fact that sunlight was far less relevent to the performance of factory work than it is to agriculture. Perhaps this custom of working 10 to 12 hours 6 days per week survived as long as it did because agriculture continued to be the norm for more than half the population until the 1900s—hence the standard for all the country's inhabitants. There can be little doubt that the custom was abetted by the continued waves of nineteenth-century immigrants, eager to work at low wages and under otherwise miserable conditions.

Finally, during the 1920s, some progress was made toward achieving greater leisure for common working people. The average worker in manufacturing put in just over 44 hours during a 6-day week. By 1929, some slight progress had also been made toward the establishment of the 5-day week—5 percent of all workers had Saturday off.

This tentative step toward deliberately increased leisure for all was interrupted by the Great Depression. A widespread catastrophe, the Depression added varying amounts of undesired leisure through job dislocation, but did not encourage employers to lessen their demands from those still employed. If anything, the Depression probably buttressed the work ethic, which had wavered in the face of the twenties' prosperity.

Once again, it became a matter of getting what work we, as a people, could get in order to eat and be clothed. One worked *hard* because one *had to* . . . one worked hard because *that's what a person did with his adult life* if he could get work.

Despite itself, however, the Depression made a perverse contribution to leisure. There weren't enough jobs to go around. This situation led to the 5½-day week, encouraged by the Walsh-Healey Act, which forced employers to pay overtime under certain circumstances, thereby encouraging further hiring at straight time.

World War II created overdemand, often required long hours, and gave the work ethic one last push. When the war ended, steps were taken to avert another depression, leading to a 5-day week.

Between 1950 and 1960, the average workweek for all privately employed nonagricultural employees was shortened by 1 hour and 12 minutes. Between 1960 and 1970, another hour and 24 minutes had been shaved off—17 minutes a day—leaving this group with a *working* time of 37 hours and 20 minutes per week. The situation among people engaged in manufacturing, however, did not follow such a pattern. Their workweek *lengthened* slightly between 1960 and 1970, according to the Bureau of Labor Statistics.

It is fairly obvious that our progress toward a better working life has ceased. If anything, we are regressing.

Having quantified one of the effects of the 8-Day Week on average working times, it may be appropriate to discuss how a variety of job functions might be performed. These have been broadly classified as being essentially clerical activities, personal selling activities, closely related intercompany activities, manufacturing, and upper management functions.

As a general rule, continuity and communication are the keys to maintaining a smooth flow of business both within and among companies. Without these elements, our business lives would become insufferably chaotic. This premise is one of the major reasons for suggesting earlier that one-eighth of the work force should start their 4-day work cycle each morning of the 8-Day Week and another one-eighth should start their 4-day rest cycle each evening. The mechanics of this system can be seen in the visualization below. In it, each of the cycle groups represents an eighth of either a single firm's employees or the total work force, however you want to look at it. The block in which each letter (denoting a cycle group) lies represents four calendar days. You can see from this picture that "A"s can talk to everyone but "B"s, "C"s with everyone but "D"s, and so on.

Days of the year

1 2 3 4 5 6 7 8 9 10 11 12 13 14 15 16 17 18 19 20 21 22 23 24 25 26 27 28 29➔

Cycle groups

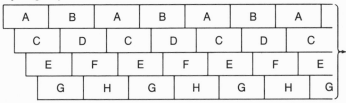

Most firms operate on the basis of chains of command involving supervisors and those who report to them. That being the case, it is clearly desirable, wherever possible, to arrange employees' schedules so that vertical communication is maintained. In the picture, then, "A"s and "B"s would have roughly equal if not identical status on the organization chart, and have less need to communicate with each other than with those shown directly below them. Put another way, both A and B could provide coverage for each other when one of them is absent and their underlings require guidance or other leadership assistance.

It looks and sounds fairly complicated, and it is, particularly in the abstract manner in which the concept is presented here. The idea will be easier to grasp if you think of it in terms of your own job situation and after reading the description of how the 8-Day Week would apply to several types of businesses.

Many people work in situations which basically rely on maintenance of good records.

Banks typify this neatness syndrome. Every day, tellers start with a given sum of money, checked to be certain of the total, then proceed to carry out their function as check cashers, money changers, and handlers of deposits and withdrawals. At the end of the day, each teller sums up his day's activities, reaching a net balance, stemming from these activities, of zero—that is, he is able to account for every dime going in and out and is prepared to adjust the customers' and bank's books accordingly. In turn, the cashier, and/or bank manager, totals the sum of the tellers' activities together with those of loan officers and themselves, and, in essence, closes the books. This process takes place every day in every bank, going one step further in the case of branches that report their activities to a central office, which then "closes" its books—generally assisted by computers programmed to handle a welter of detail accurately.

Careful, up-to-date records are kept, therefore, not only regarding the bank's over-all activities and position but also regarding the status of their customers, big and small, corporate or individual.

For such an operation, it is a fairly simple matter to spread the work from a 5-day cycle to a constant activity while maintaining smooth intracompany communications.

If a customer wishes to discuss a personal loan, there's a loan officer there to see what can be done. If it's a matter requiring loan committee action, such committees *already* meet only on certain days, rather than every business day, hence no change at all is necessary. In all but the smallest banks, there are several people trained and equipped to do identical functions, e.g., tellers or loan officers. These people can be called alter egos in the context of their functions. By scheduling these people along the lines outlined earlier (A versus B, C versus D, etc.), the banking *functions* can be covered and adequately staffed to handle a customer load which has been spread over 7 days per week rather than 5. Within the bank itself, it's a simple matter to communicate with your alter ego regarding what's happening—loan status, personnel decisions, etc.—by means of memoranda (handwritten, taped, or typed). As further protection against slip-ups, there would exist the communications bridge provided by other commonly interested employees. This can be demonstrated by showing how part of the A, B, C, D picture illustrated earlier could look in terms of maintaining communications. In this case, E and F work alternately and variously for A and B:

Days of the week

	M T W Th F Sa Su	M T W Th F Sa Su	M T W Th F Sa Su	M T W Th F Sa Su	M T W
Mr. A*	X X X X	X X X X	X X X X	X X X X	
Ms. B*	X X X X	X X X X	X X X X	X X X
Ms. E†	X X X X	X X X X	X X X X	X X X X
Ms. F†	X X	X X X X	X X X X	X X X X	X

*Functional equivalents
†Their secretaries

The theory, value, and application of the communication bridge applies, to varying degrees, in other relationships to maintain continuity, dialogue, and momentum—fitting in, as it does, with mass employers' essentially vertical chains of command.

There are other, basically clerical activities which depend on good control of constantly received inputs to survive. Individuals in such businesses would need an alter ego as bankers would. The stockbroker is such an example. He too must be neat to a fare-thee-well, executing orders immediately when requested to do so or keeping track of functions which must *potentially* be done, such as "buy or sell *at* such and such a price." He must, therefore, keep his records assiduously.

In addition, stockbrokers perform other functions aside from advising customers and executing transactions. They frequently develop specialized knowledge of certain industries, act as advisers to companies, seek information from officers of companies in which they may have present or potential investment interest, etc. All of these activities may require a broker's absence, from time to time, during working days. To accommodate these conflicting demands, a broker *already has* an alter ego to cover him during such absences.

When you call up your broker and he's not there, you and your money aren't left hanging. Provision has been made for the broker in the next office to assist.

Under the 8-Day Week, this already extant system could simply be permanently formalized. You would have two brokers to execute your directives at any given moment, two brokers to advise you orally if you need more information or reassurance than can be gleaned from the brokerage house's newsletters and other available market oracles—but only one broker at a time.

There are other examples of files-oriented activities which could be easily adapted to a constant business cycle, including the post office, the stock and commodity exchanges, and race tracks.

Activities which require more or less regular coverage of a number of clients in order to maintain relationships and sell products are a somewhat more difficult problem, but not insoluble.

Take Joe, salesman for the Heavier Paperweight Company. Joe's 5-day territory could have comprised either all of upstate New York, certain companies there, or one major account. In any of these situations, Joe made a certain number of personal contacts as required to maintain or increase his company's position relative to competition and his own position relative to other salesmen— especially Harvey down the hall, with whom Joe maintains a friendly rivalry.

Under the new regime, Joe's (and Harvey's) function can be reorganized in a number of ways, one of which should meet his own, his company's, and his clients' needs. He can either (1) keep his territory and service intact and unto himself by making more calls per hour than formerly, thus approximating his former coverage level; (2) share his clients with Harvey, and vice versa, thereby *increasing effective* client coverage in terms of employing a wider variety of personalities and sales approaches; or (3) work out some modification of (2) in which both he and Harvey keep certain highly productive clients or relationships to themselves, avoid personalities with whom they lack effectiveness or rapport, and share the rest.

In all of these examples, Joe and Harvey would most likely be scheduled on directly opposite cycles—if one were an "A" the other would be a "B"—in reflection of the fact that they are alter egos to all intents and purposes. Opposite scheduling of these individuals gives the paperweight company the manpower it requires to meet daily sales needs as they occur. It is as difficult to generalize about salesmen as it is to do so regarding the millions of other job functions which the country's population performs. Some salesmen never leave the office, doing all their work by phone. This type fits in most easily with the 8-Day Week's concept since their activities tend to be both dehumanized due to lack of personal contact and, perhaps, of an order-taking nature. On the other hand, there are salesmen who are rarely in the office, who spend virtually all their time out calling on customers. Such people do not fit neatly into the concept of the 8-Day Week inasmuch as they *already* tend to make their own hours and days, justifying their employment to management by their selling performance. It is possible that such people would actually become more productive under the 8-Day Week due to their need for mobility (reduced road traffic increases travel speed and reduces fatigue) and a reduction in their travel time in relation to actual selling time in the context of formally lengthened hours on workdays.

Even if Joe and Harvey are presently unequal as producers, a fair means of rewarding their respective efforts can be worked out through a system of average-income maintenance, bonus adjustments, and other delicate instruments available to management.

Again, where working communication between these two field men must take place, there are always memos, the boss, secretaries, or assistants who would be overlapped to provide continuity within the basic A, B, C, D framework established earlier.

Certain types of business require two or more companies to work together very closely on projects or products in which they share strong common interest. A good example of such tandem activity can be found in the functionings of companies that manufacture something for purchase and use, or consumption (hereafter the Client), and companies whose business it is to help ensure the product's consumption (hereafter the Advertising Agency). This process often requires close and frequent communications to the point that members of the two types of companies tend to behave as though they both worked for the same employer. In a sense, they do, since they bend their common effort to increasing acceptance and consumption of the product or service with which they are concerned. This shared interest and activity leads to the establishment of a *series* of complicated interrelationships both within and among the firms concerned with the activity at hand. The 8-Day Week could work within such a complicated and delicate setup. Amalgamated Viands, our Client company, makes two brands of margarine, plus a tub version of one, chocolate (candy), chocolate (cooking), chocolate (hot and instant), tea (loose, bags, plus a variety of instants), flour, "better" flour, leavened flour with premixed baking ingredients, syrup and molasses, soft drink mixes, desserts and puddings, breakfast cereals (thirty kinds), breakfast cereal substitutes (solid), breakfast cereal substitutes (liquid when mixed with milk), and fifty other products too unimportant to mention. Amalgamated Viands is a large and varied company.

They employ 65,000 people in their factories and logistics departments, 2,500 in sales and sales service personnel among their numerous divisions, and 3,300 people in the home office whose functions range from chairman, through division general managers, to group product managers, product managers, associate and assistant product managers, trainees, and secretaries.

Such a large company usually retains one or more large advertising agencies to assist it in successfully presenting its products to consumers. Within such agencies there necessarily exists a fairly complicated hierarchy of employees, all of whom are concerned with performing different aspects of the advertising function for one or more of the hypothetical Amalgamated Viands products. Among those concerned are account supervisors, account executives, and assistant account executives, who perform the dual roles of co-ordinating other agency personnel's activity on behalf of the product and serving as prime interlocutors between Client and Agency. Other Agency personnel involved include copywriters, who actually write the ads; art directors, who imagine and execute the ads' visual aspect; research experts, whose function it is to evaluate the ads' effectiveness; and many, many other specialists.

The involvement of so many people at both Client and Agency sides breeds a complicated situation—and the need to communicate, as well as to hold numerous meetings, becomes virtually paramount. Nonetheless, the 8-Day Week can be successfully applied to it. It works reasonably well, because both organizations are vertically organized hierarchies, and because A through H cycling offers considerable workday overlap among those concerned with marketing our imaginary product.

An example of how these people can perform their functions (with emphasis on holding meetings) deals with middle management and those reporting to them. In this case, Client middle management is the group product manager, who is responsible for several Amalgamated Viands brands. Reporting to him in this example are two product managers, each of whom is concerned with one brand, and their assistants. The Agency portion of the example also starts at the middle management level, i.e., the account supervisor, who is also concerned with providing advertising functions for several brands. Under him are the account executives, each concentrating on one product, and their assistants. Upper management for both Client and Agency are omitted here for two reasons: (1) the effect of the 8-Day Week on upper management is dealt with separately later in the chapter; and (2) most of the day-to-day meetings and activities carried on in this interface situation take place from middle management downward.

The Client and Agency people involved at this level day to day can be shown, with omissions for simplicity's sake, to be arrayed in such a way as to allow for meetings, telephone discussions, preparation time for these meetings, time to assemble data and write rationales for points of view, etc. As can be seen from the following cycle chart, even the lowliest assistant whatsit gets the opportunity for exposure to his superiors, and everybody has increased opportunity for housekeeping, including the topmost people shown, who under present circumstances are so pressed by their subordinates that they have very little time available for communication with *their* superiors.

It is interesting to note in the chart that although interrelationships were arranged to meet the dual needs of getting the work done and enabling commonly involved individuals to hold meetings, the combined work forces of the two companies are almost

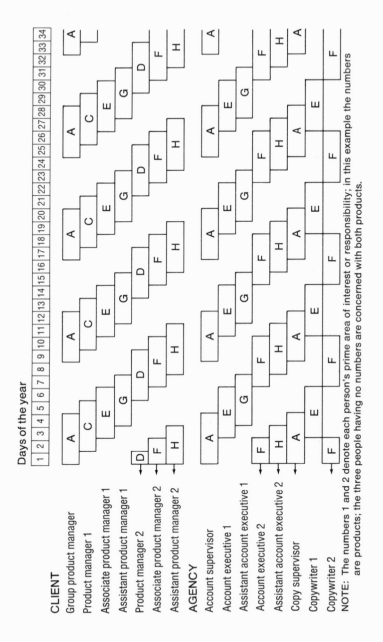

Days of the year

	1	2	3	4	5	6	7	8	9	10	11	12	13	14	15	16	17	18	19	20	21	22	23	24	25	26	27	28	29	30	31	32	33	34

CLIENT

Group product manager

Product manager 1

Associate product manager 1

Assistant product manager 1

Product manager 2

Associate product manager 2

Assistant product manager 2

AGENCY

Account supervisor

Account executive 1

Assistant account executive 1

Account executive 2

Assistant account executive 2

Copy supervisor

Copywriter 1

Copywriter 2

NOTE: The numbers 1 and 2 denote each person's prime area of interest or responsibility; in this example the numbers are products; the three people having no numbers are concerned with both products.

evenly spread over time. The blank spaces would be filled by employees of both companies who are not shown, but whose job levels and functions would be similar to those shown in this skeleton example.

The preceding example may be an exercise in tedium, but it does demonstrate how *even the most complicated sets of business relationships can be adapted to the 8-Day Week.*

Manufacturing tends to be the least individualized of the types of activities people undertake to earn a living. As such, it lends itself most easily of all to revised scheduling. Within this over-all context of simplicity, however, there exists an enormous number of differences in functional detail from industry to industry and company to company.

This and the fact that the 8-Day Week involves the presence of one-half of a company's total complement on a given day, imply that workers may have the opportunity to perform different functions at various times instead of being limited to endless repetition of a single activity throughout each workday.

"Stretching"—reduced boredom and/or refreshment-through-variety—is assuming ever-increasing importance to a labor force that is becoming continually younger, better educated, and somewhat more sophisticated in identifying its job-related needs. The following on the subject, taken from the *New York Times*, is typical:

What the company is discovering is that workers not only want to go back to the pre-October pace, but many feel that the industry is going to have to do something to change the boring, repetitive nature of assembly line work or it will continue to have unrest at the plant.

An official familiar with the sessions said, "What they're saying is you've got to do something. I don't know what it is, but you've got to do something."

Whenever the change to the 8-Day Week requires worker "stretching," the amorphous "something" mentioned in this article will be happening.

There are several varieties of upper management that bear consideration in the context of the 8-Day Week. These include officers
of business firms (board chairmen, presidents) and civic leadership
(mayors, police commissioners). Some of these management types
lend themselves well to the system, others do not, due either to
circumstances or to their already established and abnormal work
habits.

Let's begin with corporate upper management. It should be
pointed out that extremely broad variances exist in management
procedure, decision-making processes, and operational makeup between Company A and Company Z. Some presidents run their
companies by fiat and ukase, from time to time telling the directors
what they have done. Some presidents do *what they are told* to do
by the chairman and directors, or *do what is recommended* by their
underlings after reviewing such recommendations with everyone.
Some presidents don't get around much while others resemble per-
petual motion—not merely out of the office, town, and state but
frequently out of the country, in pursuit of a stunning array of
objectives and agendas. As a result, a suitable adaptation to the
8-Day Week will: (1) represent a tailor-made solution built by the
individuals themselves to meet their companies' and their own
needs, and (2) probably not bear any more resemblance to the
neat rhythm of The Alternative than their current work schedules
do to a 5-day 40-hour week.

It seems fair to suggest that there are as many or more chief
executives and other members of uppermost management where
they are today *because they are gluttons for work* as there are for
reasons of inheritance or connections. This peculiar makeup leads
them to work when and as they like. They make their own hours,
paying little attention to the clock. For these people, formal weekends and formal vacation-taking are matters of decidedly secondary
importance. They take time off when they feel they can—perhaps
to spend four days in Canada, fishing and talking business, to
wedge in a few days in Europe around a business trip, or to take

a quick journey to Barbados some Wednesday afternoon for a long weekend. Such is a normal pattern of relaxation for members of upper corporate management.

Nonetheless, a neat pattern can be worked out for top management, involving uneven cycling, in which these people would work 5 days, then take 3 days off, to allow for meetings among *everyone* involved at the top every 4 days.

Whatever adjustments may be made in top management as a result of cycling, whatever requirements a given company may have, it can be done. If a company is now an autocracy, the autocrat can continue to work himself as hard as he has in the past, forbidding major decision making in his absence, thus carrying the same load he has always borne. In more common cases, where the act of reaching a decision is a shared and evolutionary process, the alternating-box, meeting-overlap system provides a rough basis for refinement to meet particular needs. In *any* case, it should be pointed out that *major corporate decisions are not made every day;* hip-shooting is anathema to the big-company scheme of things, and decisions are made after considerable documentation, questioning, rationalizing, discussion, absorption, reconsideration, and repeated avoidance of the decision itself. This means that the need for upper management's presence at work every day could be considered to be less vital in terms of creating work stoppage than the presence of lower-echelon workers would be.

Members of top management can and will take care of themselves, arranging matters so that the decision-making process becomes no worse, if not actually better, than things now stand in this regard.

Mayors, police chiefs, and high-level firemen are a different, and simpler, matter. They and their functions adapt very easily to The Alternative.

The police, fire, and other departments are organized in such a way as to be able to react automatically to major outside stimuli. Chains of command are fairly clear-cut and stratified. As a result, a deputy police chief or chief inspector will tend to react the same way a police chief or commissioner would to a major problem—a riot, a monstrous traffic jam, or the question of how to whisk the President from airport to banquet should he decide to drop in. Policies, strategies, and tactics have been long developed to cover every major exigency imaginable by city management and administrative heads, thus reducing the need for special ad hoc decision-making. Added to this situation is the fact that cities already run 7 days a week and are already administered on that basis. Thus, they have already evolved and have in operation a work/rest pattern resembling the 8-Day Week's pattern of constant operation.

Depending on the size of the city, mayors have one or more deputies whose function it is to reduce his honor's decision-making load and fill in a hopelessly overloaded social–public relations calendar. If something sudden, terrible, or wonderful should happen, the deputy mayor can: (1) make the appropriate words— take the necessary action; (2) release the mayor's telephoned statement made in absentia; or (3) await the mayor's return. The following quote from the *New York Times* helps this supposition achieve the status of fact:

Mayor Lindsay said yesterday that his political campaign trips around the country were not hindering his effectiveness in running New York City.

The reason, he said, is "because I have a cabinet which is the best in the country" . . .

"And they are delivering and working harder than ever," he said. . . .

"You mean," someone finally asked, "that you leave the city to help it?"

"Yes," Mr. Lindsay said.

There are few surprises in city management—city hall already knows, pretty much, both *that* the cops, garbagemen, firemen, and subway workers will go on strike and *when* these calamities will likely occur. The city, in other words, won't go away if the mayor's out of town for a few days.

Having given examples of how the work could continue to be done in a variety of 8-Day Week applications, it might be appropriate to explore certain real and potential benefits inherent in this system and as yet unmentioned. Our recent lack of progress toward shorter working hours has been paralleled by increasing difficulty in getting to and from work. No matter where we live, most of us face the certainty every morning that the trip to work will be filled with obstacles and frustrations. However we travel, the end of the journey will probably see us emerge in an altered state of mind after having spent too much of our morning energies in merely reaching it.

Under the 8-Day Week, the number of people traveling to and from work would be reduced by half compared to present usage levels. With half as many people using all forms of transportation, the scale and frequency of traffic jams and other causes of delay should be reduced sharply, if not eliminated altogether.

Through better management of transportation facilities relative to the total working population, we would arrive at work more quickly and more refreshed. Parking would be easier and less expensive. Derelict mass transportation equipment, vulnerable as it is to breakdown and chain-reaction delays, could be retired. We could become more confident regarding how long a trip from point to point would take, less nervous about lateness, and less aggressive about getting there. These improvements amount to turning the tables on the less-for-more syndrome in which we currently find ourselves.

The 8-Day Week offers another way to cut down on the time we waste on work-related travel. We currently work approximately 240 days per year—with each workday accompanied by the trip to and from. If it currently takes you an hour to make this trip each way each working day, you are spending 480 hours per year going to and from work—the equivalent of sixty 8-hour working days. The Alternative reduces the number of workdays from 240 to 180, hence the number of work-related trips by 120 (60 fewer workdays times 2 trips a day) over the course of a year. If each trip takes an hour, you will save the equivalent of fifteen 8-hour workdays in avoided travel time. A 15-day reduction in annual commuting time is fairly impressive in and of itself. It becomes even more impressive when one considers that these weeks are currently frittered away in useless 1-hour pieces.

The above example of how we could save significant amounts of time by adopting The Alternative is felt to be a fair one. It takes something like an hour to go forty blocks by bus in New York during rush hours. Many of us take *more* than an hour getting to and from work each day. The 8-Day Week will minimize such meaningless extravagance with our *unpaid* travel time, by getting more for less out of the relationship between the amount of time we spend commuting versus actually working.

On another positive note, there is a major opportunity inherent in the suggested 4-on, 4-off pattern, namely the development of individual and aggregate ability beyond current levels . . . a chance, in essence, to realize a quantum jump in average skills and collective knowledge among our 80 million employed.

Obviously, a person who has 4 free days in a row, and is dissatisfied with his job, has a ready-made opportunity to acquire a new skill which is either better paying or otherwise more gratifying.

Four days in a row is a long time. It is sufficient time for a person to become legitimately involved in a secondary pursuit, including career-related learning processes. Millions of people today are trapped in their job and income levels, with no real reason to hope for escape or substantial improvement in their life styles before they die. Should such people discover new needs and new interests relatively late in life, at a point where they have become burdened with responsibilities, their chances of major adjustment are severely limited. For them, a clear-cut and painful decision must be made between material needs, which have become a habitual part of life, and a growing aesthetic or psychological need, which is the cause of their unrest.

Under the existing work schedule, the options are to either: (*a*) keep working and go to night school to learn a new trade or become better educated; (*b*) quit working and become a full-time student for however long is required; (*c*) give up. It is hard to do (*a*) because that route requires enormous energy and dedication. It is hard to do (*b*) because that approach holds tremendous financial obstacles. It is hard to do (*c*) because (*c*) perpetuates frustration and encourages further job alienation. The 5-day workweek, in other words, tends to shut out those who would improve themselves.

Under The Alternative, the reverse is true. People who feel the need to improve themselves as a commodity in the labor market can actually become full-time students while continuing to hold full-time jobs, without overdoing it one way or another in the process. Those whose ambition goes beyond limited credentials-building, who desire to expand the mold in which they find themselves cast, can do so, because the 8-Day Week would bring that objective within reach.

This benefit, stemming from the creation of meaningful rest cycles, is a fairly obvious one. There are additional benefits stemming from the 4-on, 4-off rhythm which are perhaps less obvious but equally important to the way we do our work.

Consider, for example, the great variety of technocrats whose economic existence is based on their ability to apply knowledge and technique to the solution of problems which won't stay solved, because times and circumstances change.

The promise of 4 days off at frequent and regular intervals offers such people a chance to do a little catching up, as well as the energy required to do so. In *Future Shock*, Alvin Toffler quotes Dr. Robert Hilliard of the Federal Communications Commission, who illustrates the growth rate of knowledge, as well as the difficulty of staying anywhere near abreast, in this manner:

At the rate at which knowledge is growing, by the time the child born today graduates from college, the amount of knowledge in the world will be four times as great. By the time that same child is fifty years old, it will be thirty-two times as great, and 97 percent of every-thing known in the world will have been learned since the time he was born.

Dr. Hilliard raises the prospect of unimagined levels of special-ism—leading to a situation in which cross-communication among different disciplines will become increasingly difficult to the point of possible extinction. The availability of substantial amounts of time, regularly spaced, would help make it possible for the techno-crat to do two things which current working custom discourages. First, the 8-Day Week will allow time for self-rejuvenating study *within* a given discipline, enabling an individual to remain more informed, hence more skilled at his specialty. The achievement of a higher average level of expertise among individuals engaged in a given area of activity will lead to further and faster development of technique within that area as a whole. Second, the opportunity to inform oneself of what's happening in related, but not identical, fields will allow for greater communication and cross-pollination of ideas, hence far greater innovation, than is possible under the current pressure of specialized knowledge's growth on the one hand and the shrinkage in assimilation time on the other. The field of medicine may be a good example of a potential beneficiary.

Another work-related implication lies within the concept of the 8-Day Week. It may be subtler than the opportunity to keep abreast of developments, but it is no less significant. You might describe it as intellectual mulching, or chewing our mental cuds—taking the time to assimilate a welter of workaday information.

We spend too much time these days reacting under pressure to a wide variety of stimuli, and too little time standing back from our work to view it objectively. Under current circumstances, this is not surprising. The pressure for decision making appears to be in-creasing. This situation tends to diminish the decision maker's time for consideration, to distort his perspective, thus diluting the quality of a series of decisions. Poor-quality decisions made today will create the subsequent need to redecide the same issue later, in an attempt to repair the damage done by the earlier mistake or inadequacy. Thus we develop a phenomenon of creating more work due to the fact that we already have too much to handle.

In *Future Shock,* Alvin Toffler identifies part of this problem as "decision stress." Here is part of what he has to say on the subject:

> The accelerative thrust and its psychological counterpart, transience, force us to quicken the tempo of private and public decision-making. New needs, novel emergencies and crises demand rapid response.
>
> Yet the very newness of the circumstances brings about a revolutionary change in the nature of the decisions they are called upon to make. The rapid injection of novelty into the environment upsets the delicate balance of "programmed" and "non-programmed" decisions in our organizations and our private lives.

Whereas our decision-response becomes less and less programmable because of the need for tailor-made decisions, our conditioning to this worsening situation has to become increasingly automatic. We become overused decision machines ready to respond, however inadequately, when our buttons are pushed. We develop a reflex called *deciding* at the cost of subordinating another, sometimes desirable, often necessary process called *thinking*.

The Alternative comprises a means of continuing the process of making decisions under fire, offset by the regular opportunity to let job-related inputs jell in our minds. As such, it promises a qualitative improvement in the millions of job-related decisions made daily. Since millions of decisions *are* made daily, this qualitative improvement should make itself cumulatively apparent within a short time. Thus, those of us who are released from our present decision-making bind will benefit personally, while contributing to the value of the sum total.

Questions of attitude toward work, or job alienation, may also be worth raising here. Many of us have jobs worth hating. It was pointed out earlier that reorganization of our time would allow those who wished to change their working situations greater potential for doing so. As pleasant and true as that may sound, the fact probably remains that the overwhelming majority of workers alienated by their working circumstances will stick in their grooves despite an increased opportunity to change.

The reasons underlying such "groove-making" may center around habit, feelings of security, and monetary considerations. Perhaps an auto worker offers a good example of such a syndrome. He does something over and over on an assembly line, killing his mind without respite and building resentment with every bolt he tightens and knuckle he bruises.

This resentment may express itself in the form of strikes or other job actions on the group level or an individual's deliberately shoddy production. Such a person has a valid reason for negative actions under current circumstances, that is, the lack of options open to him. Under the new system the malcontented worker will have less room to hide. Instead, he will be encouraged by an altered situation to face the question of self more squarely than at any time in his mature life. He will have the *alternative* of resigning himself to his current way of life, his work pattern, income and social level, or doing something about *changing* these elements. More than ever before, it will be his decision.

If a person has the time to dwell on his situation and the alternatives possibly open to him, he might decide it's just as well to maintain the status quo as far as education, job, pay, and friends go.

Having come to terms with himself, he should become better adjusted at work as well as at home; more content with his lot; less likely to deliberately produce poorly; less likely to engage in negative job-related activities; more positive in thought and action.

Having the alternative to *not* improve oneself is something worth having.

4 Some Private Matters

■

Assimilating the Facts; Knowing Ourselves and Understanding Others; Romance; Marriage; Children; Divorce

There is a growing discrepancy between the amount of effort we put into our existences and the life dividends yielded by this effort. Cheering up because things could be worse isn't going to make things better. Facing certain realities, on the other hand, may.

To this point, discussion has been limited to facing mechanical facts which make up the framework of our lives, ranging from the unpleasant realities of dirt, headaches, and the ghastly cost of adding more of the artifacts of modern life, to the encouraging truth that we can do our jobs and earn a living far more easily and logically than we currently do. Such prime realities had to be dealt with before other, more important facts of life could be explored.

These more important facts have to do with questions of self, and our ability to give and get the good that can be part of our lives.

Our individuality is under tremendous attack these days. The result is that we don't live up to anything approaching our potential as individuals, nor are we doing any better en masse. Mr. Toffler sums up the situation this way in *Future Shock:*

It is impossible to produce future shock in large numbers of individuals without affecting the rationality of the society as a whole. Today, according to Daniel P. Moynihan, [then] the Chief White

House advisor on urban affairs, the United States exhibits the qualities of an individual going through a nervous breakdown. For the cumulative impact of sensory, cognitive or decisional overstimulation, not to mention the physical effects of neural or endocrine overload, creates sickness in our midst. "This sickness is increasingly mirrored in our culture, our philosophy, our attitude toward reality. It is no accident that so many people refer to the world as a 'madhouse.' . . ."

Mr. Toffler pursues his point with these further observations:

Millions sense the pathology that pervades the air, but fail to understand its roots. These roots lie not in this or that political doctrine, still less in some mystical core of despair or isolation presumed to inhere in the "human condition." Nor do they lie in science, technology, or legitimate demands for social change. They are traceable, instead, to the uncontrolled, non-selective nature of our lunge into the future. They lie in our failure to direct, consciously and imaginatively, the advance toward super-industrialism.

Fair enough. But this is no more than an adequate description of our current situation, which, in context, may be said to hinge on the 5-day workweek and the little weekend leftovers that go with it. These weekends, these vestiges of time, really are not adequate to the task of letting us *be* consciously imaginative about our continual entry into the future, or even of equipping ourselves to deal with last week's problems. Were we commonly able to enjoy 4 days of regular leisure after each 4 days of concentrated work, we could achieve an estate which is currently the exclusive domain of two small segments of society—the very wealthy and those who have turned their backs on the generally accepted concept of normal adult behavior. Rich people, by dint of their wealth, are in a position to do as they wish with their time. They are free to pursue whatever objectives or diversions they may please, free of care as to where the money necessary to sustain life is coming from. Whether they avail themselves of it or not, such moneyed individuals have the opportunity to use time as a means of achieving goals relating to such amorphous personal elements as understanding oneself and achieving peace of mind.

Those who reject the commonly accepted norm of working regularly for a living by "dropping out" also enjoy a considerable amount of leisure time and can avail themselves of its fruits to a far greater degree than the average working adult. The only way this latter group can do so, however, is by dropping money out of their personal equations. They tend to exchange cars, houses, and color television sets for the time to live their own lives as they see fit. Such a decision is directly related to the concept that "time is money." Since the average man must steadily pursue money if he is to possess the normal artifacts of wealth, it can also be said that "money is time." The dropout has reached that realization and made a decision to keep his time for his own use.

Most of us do not feel free to make such a decision. Therefore most of us cannot currently aspire to the luxury of time, or its benefits.

The 8-Day Week gives us the time we have never had, and will never have, as long as our lives are governed by a 5-day work-week. The rest of this chapter is devoted to the meaning time can have to our lives once we have learned to allocate it in such a way as to make the personal portion as usable as that portion which is devoted to earning a living.

Consider our status as individuals today. More than ever, we need security bred of inner stability. In the past, we could hide under a "borrowed stability" by maintaining roles within a structure. We lived in a neighborhood, belonged to a church, had a job, and rooted for the home team. We were Americans, knew what that meant, and loved it. Our sense of self was fostered by the rate of social change, which crept along imperceptibly and virtually unnoticed. This situation made it comfortable for us to go through counterfeit motions of individual expression, when in reality we were reflecting group attitudes in microcosm.

Such borrowed individualism and stability has now become impossible. Neighborhoods evaporate, churches seem less relevant to real life, jobs are where we get money, and the home team has moved to San Diego or Hackensack. We can't even conform to attitudes and images, because they won't stand still. Consider F.D.R. as an image. A person could maintain an impression of him over a dozen years because, during that time, his image didn't alter substantially. Now consider the gamut of meanings which these words have run in rapid succession: Republican party; (no longer red) China; Vietnam. These are established, important "facts"; yet they undergo constant revisions in meaning. To these are added a welter of new facts in the form of philosophies and their authors, who themselves undergo continual change; for example, the Beatles, as opposed to John Lennon, George Harrison, Paul Mc-Cartney, and Ringo Starr.

The need on the part of individuals to understand and assimilate the continually new meanings of people's names, countries, and philosophies is not eased by the fact that peer groups, of which these individuals are members, continue to exist. The sheer quantity of new inputs requiring relatively immediate assimilation makes it impossible to await group interpretation and dissemination to a dependent membership. As the mass of information and interpretations increases, the time for emotional and mental digestion of these data is decreasing. The Alternative carries with it a provision for meeting such individually oriented exigencies. It would allow considerable opportunity to hear what is being said, to see what is happening, and assign meanings to this information. The result would be the development of *individuals* in a more genuine sense, rather than millions of *unattached persons* who lack both moorings and bearings. The deliberate encouragement of our ability to think and understand should yield two types of dividends: individual insecurity will diminish in the face of greater confidence, which is gained by investigating and dealing with the unknown; greater self-confidence and clearer thinking will encourage better communication among individuals and groups.

Not long ago, a disastrous failure to communicate took place between large numbers of nonestablishment youth and established middle age. Both sides in this attempted dialogue suffered from an inability to articulate their positions. Such a failure might be said to have stemmed as much from an inability on the part of participants to establish clearly in their own minds what their objectives were as from other differences which may have existed between them, as in vocabulary, dress, and general deportment. The resulting failure to communicate led to clash.

The bloodletting and foundation shaking which accompanied this disastrous failure to communicate has subsided. The potential for its renewal, however, continues. It continues in the minds of those members of the establishment who find it more convenient to react than to take the time to consider, and it continues in the minds of antiestablishment elements whose tactics appear to have changed from confrontation to infiltration.

Members of these opposing and noncommunicating elements must come to a better understanding of the importance, worth, and unavoidable interrelationship between each other's contrasting values. Until this happens, we are all sitting on a bomb. The bomb will not go away until individual fear is replaced by self-confidence, and we start talking to each other.

It is possible that such an increased ability to communicate can come from increased opportunity for introspection, particularly on the part of the establishment side of the conflict. This feeling is not based on a partisan criticism of this group, but on the belief that these people tend to be more entrenched in their attitudes and less accustomed to making rapid adjustments than younger people are, as well as extremely occupied with the business of earning a living, hence lacking sufficient time for other considerations.

There are other problems which might be solved as a result of better understanding ourselves, hence others. Racial tensions, for example. When we don't even begin to understand ourselves, how on earth are we going to understand others who inhabit a world of different hue, language, customs, income, upbringing, and outlook? The black man simply *cannot* be oblivious to the white man's motivations if he is going to relate effectively to them. The white man really *cannot* ignore the existence of black emotional interests, nor can he continue to be oblivious to their origins and meaning. Neither one can continue to accept simplistic explanations of the other's motives and behavior. Both must communicate if neither is to be repeatedly bothered by feelings of guilt, inadequacy, repression, fear, jealousy, self-righteousness, and puzzlement. Too many excuses presently exist for not pausing to consider problems in communication. One basic excuse (and a valid one) is that the time to do so has been systematically preempted.

Human interrelationships across sex lines is another subject worthy of discussion. A great deal of misery, maladjustment, conflict, and expense occurs in connection with male-female relationships. In fact, such relationships, which play a very large part in our private lives, are commonly connected with leisure time. Thus, the topic would appear to bear discussion to the extent that it is relevant to this book's over-all subject.

Obviously, the 8-Day Week offers a greater opportunity to meet, enjoy, and appreciate more people than is available under the current system. Furthermore, it would appear to offer a considerably improved opportunity to become well acquainted with someone before making commitments which may ultimately prove to have been ill considered.

In the strictly arithmetical sense, The Alternative offers a 46 percent improvement over the current system in terms of offering yearly potential social encounters on nonworkdays and evenings. The theoretical maximum number of weekend dates currently available is 156, i.e., every Friday, Saturday, and Sunday evening. Applying the same full-use approach in the context of the 8-Day Week yields a potential of 228 yearly dates, or 5 out of every 8 days. Whether it is realized or not, the mathematical potential for encountering someone suited to one's own personality is therefore increased.

Of possibly greater basic importance, however, is what could happen to the weekend itself as a perception. Currently, the weekend carries with it a considerable amount of social pressure for single people. Even the "liberated" are expected to have social encounters during these days, and may go to some lengths to fulfill such expectations. In addition, *the fact of* weekends themselves constitutes a form of pressure *to enjoy* such encounters. The Alternative would essentially eliminate the weekend, as it currently takes place, by spreading leisure periods throughout the week. This act would tend to take pressure off individuals to have special dates on certain days. Such an effect is in harmony with the 8-Day Week's general thrust toward reduced pressures in all aspects of life.

Current efforts to build meaningful relationships tend to act in more or less direct defiance of modern life as it is led, and the conditioning we undergo in the process of learning to cope with it. Our attitudes and environment appear to be increasingly geared to disposability, pliability, and survival itself. The concept of deep relationships, then, could be said to conflict directly with an attitude which essentially calls for *survival through noninvolvement*.

Mechanically speaking, the current structure of work and leisure militates against those who would build deep relationships.

It seems fair to hypothesize that with greater time at their disposal for leisure activities, individuals would not only be able to gain release from work and get the chores done, but also have time remaining to better discover themselves and better understand others.

Presumably, more effective and stable relationships would result.

The effect of current work-rest patterns and the potential effect of The Alternative on romance carries through to marriage and all it connotes. The chances are heavily in favor of our all being married at least once in our lifetimes. Chances increasingly tend to favor our being married even more than once in our lifetimes, whether we like it or not. In *Future Shock,* Mr. Toffler interprets these facts along the following lines:

> The orthodox format presupposes that two young people will "find" one another and marry. It presupposes that the two will fulfill certain psychological needs in one another, and that the two personalities will

develop over the years, more or less in tandem, so that they continue to fulfill each other's needs. It further presupposes that this process will last "until death do us part."

These expectations are built deeply into our culture. It is no longer respectable, as it once was, to marry for anything but love. Love has changed from a peripheral concern of the family into its primary justification. Indeed, the pursuit of love through family life has become, for many, the very purpose of life itself.

Love, however, is defined in terms of this notion of shared growth. It is seen as a beautiful mesh of complementary needs, flowing into and out of one another, fulfilling the loved ones, and producing feelings of warmth, tenderness and devotion. Unhappy husbands often complain that they have "left their wives behind" in terms of social, educational or intellectual growth.

Partners in successful marriages are said to "grow together." This "parallel development" theory of love carries endorsement from marriage counselors, psychologists and sociologists. Thus, says sociologist Nelson Foote, a specialist on the family, the quality of the relationship between husband and wife is dependent upon "the degree of matching in their phases of distinct but comparable development."

If love is a product of shared growth, however, and we are to measure success in marriage by the degree to which matched development actually occurs, it becomes possible to make a strong and ominous prediction about the future.

It is possible to demonstrate that, even in a relatively stagnant society, the mathematical odds are heavily stacked against any couple achieving this ideal of parallel growth. The odds for success positively plummet, however, when the rate of change in society accelerates, as it now is doing. In a fast-moving society, in which the husband moves up and down a variety of economic and social scales, in which the family is again and again torn loose from home and community, in which individuals move further from their parents, further from the religion of origin, and further from traditional values, it is almost miraculous if two people develop at anything like comparable rates.

The clock, and the limits of human endurance, constitute the parameters of our weekends, perverting a time for needed rest and basic interchange into some kind of connubial decathlon. This is the atmosphere in which two people try to achieve and maintain mutual understanding and shared growth, despite a torrent of external factors and internal individual change which must be jointly weathered if a marriage is to survive. Instead, we grow apart at different rates in different directions, maintaining our mutual relations on an increasingly "official" plane as the roles of wife and husband become more political, less social, with each added degree of individual divergence. We learn how to deal with each other in the sense of negotiation, as we unlearn what we used to know about ourselves and the other person. The distortions of our marriages keep pace with those which keep taking place within our separate selves. Such social torque, if not a direct outgrowth of our present workweek, is at least strongly abetted by it. Time for repairs is limited. The marriage mechanism becomes overstrained. And, sometimes, it breaks down irreparably.

Explosive growth is taking place in the number of divorces occurring annually. Between 1960 and 1966, annual divorces rose by 27 percent; by 1970, the number of divorces taking place annually had risen by 82 percent compared to 1960 levels. During this ten-year period, as divorce increased by 82 percent, population grew by 10 percent. Divorce, then, *grew eight times as rapidly* as population. It is worth noting that these comparisons span all of a ten-year period.

Such data, along with anyone's observations within his own social and business circles, leave little doubt that marriage troubles are persistently trending upward. Among other things, divorces are expensive to those who participate in them. Exclusive of the costs of alimony and child support, and the sheer waste in money represented by maintenance of two households for the remnants of what was once a single family, stands the cost of bringing about this legal disintegration. The average cost in lawyers' fees alone is at least $1 billion annually.

Cold numbers, however, do not begin to reflect the human cost of divorce. A great deal of emotion and energy goes into the formation of a family. Divorce is a culmination of such efforts which have proved inadequate to the job, no matter how well-intended such efforts may have been. To this futile effort is added the additional strain upon newly divorced people who must begin life again, redesignated as individuals.

Whether a marriage is progressing "normally" or has ended in divorce, it generally carries with it the presence of offspring.

According to the Bureau of the Census, approximately 56 percent of U.S. households contain one or more children under 18. This over-all percentage takes no account of the fact that many households are headed by people whose children can be expected to have grown up and formed their own households. In fact, 30 percent of total households in this country are headed by people over 55. If you assume that none of these households contains a dependent child under 18, you can estimate the percentage of households headed by persons of child-bearing age by interpolation. Using this approach, it may be concluded that approximately 80 percent of younger households contain minor children.

Kids are bright. Kids are naturally loving, helpful, and eager to please. Kids will content themselves with very little, but are capable of giving a great deal. Kids are mines of imagination and wells of curiosity. They invented flower children, discovered long hair, bare feet, and bangles. They tune in, turn on, and drop out. Or, perhaps, get dropped.

The workweek, as we live it, can take a lot of credit for the way our kids turn out. It's a legitimate excuse, on the one hand, and a cruel fact, on the other, that there isn't much time in our lives for our offspring. If we go much further along our current course, our kids may literally become legitimate excuses. As we become increasingly less effective parents, we become increasingly antisocial citizens. Kids who are neurotic, because they are not loved, wind up attacking their society and requiring a different kind of attention at some future date. Kids who can't read ultimately flunk, even if they are passed from grade to grade until they enter a socioeconomy which is unprepared to carry an illiterate. Kids who can't see any meaning in their parents' treadmill existence are likely candidates to duck the system when their turn comes. If enough of them *do* duck, it spells more than a lot of individual parental disappointment; it spells economic disaster for those same parents as they look to Social Security and retirement benefits, which will not be forthcoming *unless someone continues to contribute money to such funds.*

Uncared-for kids may become uncaring kids; unfinished products; nongrownups. Four days off, in a row, after four working days, would presumably offer greater opportunity to discover the meaning of words which are fast becoming anachronisms. These words are: mother, father, son, daughter, love, family, you, me, us, we.

There is another aspect to child-rearing which appears worthy of separate discussion. This is the subculture of *divorced parents and their offspring.* Under present circumstances, it's difficult in the extreme for a mother (who probably has custody) to work, have a social life, *and* care for her children beyond seeing to it that they are clothed and fed. Work is work. It is arduous, regardless of the actual function involved. A woman who works, goes to and from her place of employment, keeps house, and tries to look and feel decent has her hands full. She must have a little escape in the form of dinner dates, movies, and concerts, weekends somehow stolen away from the sameness and drudgery of working and running a house.

These facts encourage a contradiction in her life, herself, and her children. There is the need to be a provider, which mismatches with the need to run a house. There is the need to be a person, which collides with the job of being a loving presence for unformed individuals who need shaping. There is the guilt that goes with an average human being's not being Wonder Woman.

All these contradictory elements can be said to combine against the formation of a happy, balanced person. Instead, they could be expected to result in one who is complete in many respects, unfulfilled in many ways, unhappy for a variety of reasons, and inadequate in the performance of her role as mother.

Even attempts to alleviate this situation on the part of the divorced mother may backfire. Day-care centers, which would theoretically provide great assistance to the working divorcee, are in short supply. Furthermore, those which do exist may not operate in such a way as to encourage a feeling of confidence and peace of mind on her part. In fact, they may even have the reverse effect—generating further feelings of guilt—if the following excerpts from the *New York Times* are indicative:

A day-care crisis throughout the country and a "terrifying collection" of incidents of child abuse and neglect were reported . . . after a study of nearly 700 day-care centers and homes serving 25,000 children.

The report . . . gives examples of filthy centers, "repulsive" and overcrowded conditions in private homes and exorbitant fees, which many working mothers cannot pay.

"Much of the existing care is abominable," states the section on Atlanta.

"The psychic damage to children in poor day care is frightening. We have concluded that since serious damage can be done by poor day care, in many cases no care is better."

Although divorced mothers bear the brunt of the conflicts arising between leading their own lives and rearing their children, fathers also encounter certain problems which relate to established work and leisure patterns. Mothers typically have custody, while fathers often "borrow" children for the weekend. In such a situation, mothers have two free days per week, during which they neither work nor must care for their children. The father's free time, however, is limited to those hours after work inasmuch as his weekends are committed to seeing and caring for his children. If fathers studiously devote all their weekend time to their children, they are in the position of leading a "deformed" life to the extent of being denied participation in more normal adult weekend activities. On the other hand, if they pursue such adult activities, they do so at the possible expense of their children—depending on the children's ages and the relationship which exists between father and offspring. The inclusion of another woman, or women, in this weekend situation may tend to further deteriorate a man's relationship with his children or cause various sorts of unwonted problems.

In such a situation, involving divorced and working parents with children, imaginative use of the 8-Day Week might prove helpful. The following example allows mothers more time to themselves; allows fathers more time with their children; allows both mothers and fathers a limited number of unfettered periods of leisure:

	1 2 3 4 5 6 7 8 9 10 11 12 13 14 15 16 17 18 19 20 21 22 23 24 25
Mother	works | rests | works | rests | works | rests | wor
Has charge of children	yes | no | yes | no | yes | no
Father	works | rests | works | rests | works | rests
Has charge of children	no | yes | no | yes | no | yes

5 Outgrowths of the New Leisure

■

Making Entertainment More Accessible,
Participating Activities More Rewarding,
Unaffordable Dreams Come True, and
Urban Renewal Possible

The availability of more leisure time is an appealing concept in a general way. Some specific suggestions as to its meaning, in terms of how it might be put to use fruitfully, however, would appear to be justified from several points of view: as a stimulus to the reader's own imagination; as a basis for discussing how leisure-time pursuits might be afforded by families whose means are limited; as background for speculating on a major socio-economic side effect which such leisure might yield. Thus, a train of thought having simple beginnings will lead to more complex, and less obvious, speculations as this chapter progresses.

It is possible that the conduct of major spectator sports could change significantly in reflection of a change in opportunity to attend events or to view them on television. The fact that one-half of all working people would be off on any given day would make any day as good as any other in terms of an available audience for whatever event might be offered, in contrast to the current practice of scheduling virtually everyone's leisure on weekends. A major effect could be had on professional football teams, for example. Pro football is now played for the most part on Sunday afternoons, a custom that finds its roots in its earliest days, when the game was in no position to compete for followers with more popular and better established college teams, which usually held their contests on Saturdays. Although pro football's fortunes have changed considerably since its earliest beginnings, Sunday games have persisted for several reasons, such as custom, the desirability of daytime warmth for a sport played in cold weather, the availability of large audiences on a nonworking day. Custom as a factor in determining when games will be played has already undergone some adjustment (reflecting economic considerations) in the form of occasional Saturday-night games and regular Monday-night events, both of which add to the total store of televisable action and the revenue generated by it, but weather considerations and the availability of leisure-day audiences are constant under present circumstances. If audiences were to become available for entertainment every day, professional football could adjust to, and capitalize on, this fact in at least two ways:

1. By scheduling games more frequently, e.g., every six days instead of every seven. A tighter schedule would yield two or three additional games over the course of a season. Aside from generating proportionately greater income to franchise owners and broadcast media, such rescheduling would also tend to increase the number *of different live spectators* attending a given team's games over the course of a season. This effect would result from the fact that current season-ticket holders would be prevented from attending some home games due to their being at work on certain dates. Although such a consideration may seem picayune to some, it would not be so to others. Many professional teams are sold out season after season. Those people who would like to attend games but do not hold tickets are permanently excluded. It would seem desirable from a team's point of view to increase the size of its *live* following, hence *the quality* of that following's interest and loyalty.

2. By creating two teams, in place of one, and playing a greatly expanded schedule of day games. For example, two such teams could each play a game every six days, and be scheduled three days apart. The chart below indicates that,

using this approach, spectators would have an opportunity to watch eleven games, either at home or televised, in a 31-day month, as opposed to a maximum of five games under the current system.

Days of the month

	1	2	3	4	5	6	7	8	9	10	11	12	13	14	15	16	17	18	19	20	21	22	23	24	25	26	27	28	29	30	31
Team I	X					X					X					X					X					X					X
Team II			X					X					X					X					X				X				
Current approach	X						X							X						X						X					

Although division of a team into two parts would tend to dilute the quality of play for a limited time, past experience would indicate that a sufficient amount of talent could be developed to overcome such a temporary deficiency. Drawbacks born of such expansion in schedules would doubtless be offset by a considerable increase in the size of any given team's spectator base. Questions of championship could be settled through combined records for both teams, and unified teams could hold final playoffs.

Other spectator sports might also adopt a dual-team system. Basketball and hockey teams might be in a position to field two teams, resulting in a continuous home stand, more day games, and a substantial broadening in the number of people able to obtain tickets to their events. More leisure time might also take the form of potentially greater interest in less popular sports, such as soccer, lacrosse, and Rugby, as spectators availed themselves of the opportunity to sample different entertainments.

Baseball, which is already played on a full-schedule basis, could possibly be played more often during the daytime, and draw greater numbers of parents with children as spectators.

Among other live entertainments, stage productions might relate to the presence of larger potential audiences by employing two casts and scheduling daily matinees in addition to evening performances, thus making full use of theater facilities as well as available talent. Such an approach would appear to be particularly valid in connection with extremely popular shows, for which it is often very difficult to obtain tickets under present conditions. In this arrangement, actors could work two performances daily for four days, then take four days' rest.

A substantial impact on participating activities might also be anticipated if leisure time were to constitute one-half of the year. Many individual pursuits of a sports or hobby nature are now either severely limited or rendered impossible by customary work scheduling. The time and difficulty required to enjoy certain activities are often so great as to eliminate, for many people, the pleasure they potentially offer. In a similar vein, money spent on certain hobbies may be wasted to a large extent due to the spender's inability to get his money's worth in terms of *time devoted to actual participation* in a given hobby. Urban dwellers who ski, for example, often must travel several hundred miles on dangerous and crowded roads to do so. Driving substantial distances in heavy traffic at the end of a hard workweek is tiring as well as perilous. A full day's skiing on Saturday and Sunday adds to fatigue for the long return trip on Sunday night. Those who undergo such a regimen do so at great expense in the form of renting or owning little-used living accommodations in ski areas, in addition to the cost of equipment and transportation. This situation, coupled with the fact that the slopes themselves are extremely crowded on weekends, makes skiing less rewarding than it might be.

It can be fairly speculated that adoption of the 8-Day Week might lead to a series of changes in the skier's world. The difficulty in getting to and from ski areas would be considerably lessened as traffic loads were spread across all days of the week, rather than compacted into Fridays and Sundays. Less-contentious traffic would lead to greater road safety as well as to reduced travel time between cities and mountains, along with less fatigue directly attributable to the act of traveling. On the other hand, greater opportunity to ski might lead to more skill and better conditioning on the skier's part, encouraging fewer accidents. Staggered schedules would lead to greater *average use* of available facilities, while significantly lessening present-day pressure on lifts and trails during crowded weekends. In short, skiers would enjoy more, better, and safer skiing in all respects. The mere fact that such a sport as skiing would become a more reasonable option to the winter athlete would probably lead to an increase in the number of active skiers.

What would be true of skiing would also tend to be true of all other leisure pursuits involving out-of-town travel. For example, the desire to own and use a small country property or modest farm as a refuge and a productive environment for our children would tend to be a more rational one as the time to enjoy such a retreat expanded. Those who yearn but now suppress a desire for the joys of rural life would find themselves in the position of having arguments *in favor* of such a commitment, as opposed to the phalanx of reasons which assemble *against* the notion under present circumstances. Other related and presumably wholesome aspirations might also become realities as arguments in their favor become increasingly valid. For instance, a pony or a horse might make sense for the children if they were able to make more reasonable use of such an animal than is normally possible today.

The same could be said of sailing or boating, both of which require the availability of time, as well as the investment of money, if the pleasures these activities represent to many are to be realized in proportion to the difficulties they entail. As in the case of the skier, yachtsmen would find seagoing more pleasant as weekend peak loads on marina facilities and water space were averaged across the week.

Weekend tennis players might find it reasonable to build their own courts once they found themselves free to exercise and enjoy themselves at length over regular intervals. Those who currently stand in line on weekends to play an hour, then cede the court to other, equally unsatisfied players, will find courts more readily available to them on their days off.

It may also be worth imagining what might happen to those who enjoy manual crafts as a leisure activity, and what might become of the state of their crafts, given more opportunity to practice them. People who find pleasure in a gamut of hobbies ranging from puttering around the house to intricate needlework or elaborate automobile restoration would find the potential for greater satisfaction of these urges within the 8-Day Week. John Muir has said:

> Thousands of tired, nerve-shaken, over-civilized people are beginning to find out that going to the mountains is going home; that wildness is a necessity; and that mountain parks and reservations are useful, not only as fountains of timber and irrigating rivers, but as fountains of life.

Having the time to go to, and enjoy, our respective mountains would represent a happy change from the circumstances with which many of our lives are presently surrounded. Time is only part of the question, however. Money is also involved. Almost any economist will agree that leisure time generates economic growth for the simple reason that, all in all, people tend to spend money when they are enjoying themselves. Since most of us do not enjoy a surplus of funds, how could we find the means of buying such time-related pleasures as a farm, a ski chalet, a horse? For those who feel these urges strongly enough, there is an excellent solution: cooperative living in the city during working days, and a similar sharing arrangement of the cost and fun of a given family's leisure-time interest.

Before entering into a discussion of the mechanics of how sharing might work to assist participants in achieving an upward step in their life styles, perhaps the point should be made that sharing appears to be gaining respectability and currency among mature, employed, and stable elements of our society—being no longer the exclusive province of the less established. This statement is supported by the fact of a (fairly surprising) *Wall Street Journal* article on the subject, parts of which are quoted here:

> Austin Hendrickson's home is his castle. In fact, that's what he and his family call their huge three-story house in downtown Minneapolis. It's an elegant mansion built in the 1890's, complete with redstone

exterior, copper roof and turrets. Inside are nearly two dozen rooms. . . .

. . . But Mr. Hendrickson, who is an electrician and who brings home $15,000 a year, says he isn't living beyond his means. That's because Mr. Hendrickson, his schoolteacher wife, Jean, and two of their three children share the renovated fraternity house with eight other adults and 11 children. . . .

Cooperative living is catching on among professionals, middle-aged workers and otherwise "straight" Americans.

The castle, for example, includes a tax consultant, a minister, a social worker, a university counselor and a sociologist. . . . The cooperatives usually are located in cities; and, though many of them share some features with communes, their members frequently keep their own earnings and hold in common only their living quarters. . . .

Observers attribute much of the popularity of cooperatives to economic factors. "As a single family, we just couldn't afford the kind of life-style we wanted," says Martin Adams, a 37-year-old high-school history teacher who, until last summer, lived in a $200-a-month apartment in Philadelphia. . . .

The article also points out that the trend toward cooperative living among respectable people is taking place across the country; leads to reduced costs for utilities, food, baby-sitters, and magazine subscriptions, among other things; makes robbery virtually impossible due to the constant presence of one or more adults.

Such benefits would also tend to accrue to families interested in but unable to afford an expensive leisure-related pursuit within the context of the 8-Day Week. As an example, let us suppose there are two families each now living in Manhattan on a gross income of $13,000 per year. Let us further suppose that each family has a small child, a two-bedroom apartment for which each pays $300 per month, and that each would love dearly to own a little farm somewhere well away from the city in which they work and live. These two couples could probably cooperate to advantage, somewhat along the following lines:

1. Move into a comparable three-bedroom apartment at a rent of, say, $400 per month, reflecting lower per-room costs as the size of apartments increases;

2. Let their children share a bedroom during those days when both families find themselves working in common;
3. Use the savings in rent to finance the cost of the modest farm in the woods.

In this case, the amount available for amortization of the farm's mortgage would be $200 per month—the difference between *both* their former rents ($600) and their new cooperative rent ($400). Under the 8-Day Week, it is unlikely that both families would be on identical work schedules. In fact, the odds are 7 to 1 against this happening because the entire work force would be arrayed into eight roughly equal parts (Groups A through H). On the other hand, the odds favor at least one working day and one leisure day in common for both families—and the mean would be two days together in the city and two in the country.

Were this the case, these two families would be together four days, *but only two nights*, out of every eight, since one or the other family would be departing from or returning to the city as their work cycles began or ended. In essence, then, both families would have considerable privacy under the circumstances described, while realizing their shared aspiration for a better life style.

It should be pointed out that all of the immediately foregoing is in no way a necessary part of the 8-Day Week, *but merely an illustration of how families with limited means might relate affordably* to a situation in which time comprises only half of a leisure-oriented equation. Nonetheless, the possibility of a significant increase in "cooperation" would seem to exist if circumstances were altered in such a way as to make a revised approach to certain living customs even more meaningful than simple inability to deal with spiraling living costs.

It might also be worthwhile to speculate briefly on the effect which such cooperative living could have on urban housing and related social subjects. Urban areas are beset by housing problems, particularly in poorer, ghetto areas. Many expensive, and sometimes abortive, attempts have been made to provide better, yet affordable, housing for our cities' disadvantaged. Newspapers are full of reports of the frustrations, cost, and problems encountered in the general field of urban renewal. The Federal Housing Authority, part of the U.S. Department of Housing and Urban Development, has encountered scandalous problems. In Detroit alone, efforts to improve and finance the purchase of private dwellings may result in a $100 million loss to the taxpayers, who ultimately underwrite such activities. The Detroit fiasco is expected to result in 20,000 or more foreclosures.

In the last few months, there has been a dramatic turnabout in many officials' public statements on the explosive subject of federally subsidized housing. . . . The critics say that the programs have produced a high percentage of poorly constructed housing on questionable sites at an enormous cost to the Treasury. . . .

An investigation . . . shows that housing, perhaps more than any other Federal program, is the victim of outdated institutions, insensitive government and excessive influence of special interests. . . .

Charges are beginning to be heard that the housing industry is becoming like the defense industry, dependent on Government support and thus less efficient than industries in private competition.

New York Times

Urban renewal projects, whether successful or otherwise, require a great deal of money. A cost of $10,000 per room is not extraordinary for such undertakings. It should be borne in mind, too, that such a figure is an estimated cost *of construction*, not the ultimate cost, when interest on the money used for such construction is considered. If the cost of such construction is repaid at interest over thirty years, the total price exceeds $20,000 . . . for a single room.

Aside from being expensive and poorly built, such projects also appear to fail frequently from a social viewpoint inasmuch as they are often built in slum neighborhoods or represent nothing more than transplantation of a slum to a middle-class neighborhood. In either event, a secondary objective of upgrading the people involved through assimilation into more normal—i.e., average middle-class—society tends to be missed.

The National Advisory Commission on Civil Disorders concluded after the 1967 riots that "Our nation is moving toward two societies, one black, one white—separate and unequal." The Commission pointed out that low-income housing projects were concentrated in ghettos. The New York City Housing Authority's figures indicate that, between 1966 and late 1971, only 2,647 out of 16,732 low-income dwellings built were outside slum areas.

Large-scale developments proposed for construction in middle-class neighborhoods, on the other hand, are often vigorously opposed by already established residents. The *New York Times* noted such a feeling, in part, as follows:

> They are frightened because their own not too well hidden prejudices against the poor have been fanned into new life by whispered predictions of rising crime, lowered property values and the like.

Such abysmal failure to succeed in either producing better housing or achieving some semblance of integration, and the dismally persistent urban situations which remain in being as a result, are mentioned here in the belief that the subject relates to the concept of cooperative living discussed earlier.

In the case of the two couples wishing to buy a farm, and finding the means of affording it through consolidation of their living quarters, there emerges an interesting possibility of limited urban renewal and acculturation. As each set of two families elected to merge their urban households, *one apartment would become vacant* and available for tenancy by another family. It could be that the "other family" might be from a slum—a prime candidate for "relocation" in a new slum under present circumstances. Were this the case, such a family might instead be:

1. Provided with decent housing;
2. Located in a more stable neighborhood;
3. Integrated into middle-class society.

It would seem reasonable to speculate that rent subsidies paid directly to landlords would be cheaper in the long run than financing project housing. It would also seem logical that middle-class fears regarding social distortion in their neighborhoods stemming from "project-transplants" would be lessened if such transplants took place piecemeal rather than in large, very obvious proportions.

Curiously, the process of cooperative living would not have to take place on anything resembling a massive scale to have a significant secondary effect on urban renewal. In New York City, for example, if there are an estimated total of 3 million households, a 2 percent conversion to cooperative living would generate 30,000 net available units of housing for new occupancy. This is roughly twice the number of new urban-renewal dwellings mentioned earlier in this chapter as having been erected in New York City over a six-year period.

As can be seen from the above, modest aspirations on certain individuals' parts could conceivably lead to a fairly exotic set of conclusions.

Undoubtedly, the majority of us would not find enough reasons in favor of cooperation to outweigh negative attitudes born of predictable need for privacy and pride in self-sufficiency.

Suburban dwellers might represent such an attitude in the flesh. If so, it might be appropriate to content oneself with pointing out that the 8-Day Week would offer considerable opportunity to put the theory of suburban and exurban living into actual practice. The emotional and financial investment in house, shrubs, and second cars should tend to become more rational as the opportunity to partake in the joys they represent increases.

This chapter has merely skimmed the possibilities inherent in the concept of increased leisure. Some of the speculations which emerged are, nonetheless, fairly tantalizing. Individuals considering the subject of greater leisure might be expected to find their own thoughts even more interesting than mine, because of their greater relevance and specificity.

6 Education and the 8-Day Week

■

*Using Existing Facilities; Possible Scheduling
Approaches; Possible Effects on School as a
Learning Opportunity; Free-Form Instruction;
Adolescent Development; University Students and
Professors; The Teaching Gap*

It may be supposed that one of the basic objectives of schools everywhere is to prepare youth for the day when they enter society as full-fledged contributing members. To this end, attempts are made to convey a mass of relatively finite information as a primary basis either for relating to daily life as it exists, or as a background for further educational communication of a more complex nature. Among these earlier finites are a contemporary version of the three R's, accompanied by social and attitudinal guidance which may touch on such concepts as learning to share; cooperate with others; be prepared to meet tests; organize activities in terms of priorities, and relate to fairly well established social disciplines.

If this is true, then perhaps latter stages of education encompass, to a large degree, assimilating and storing large quantities of increasingly specialized information, accompanied by continued development of the student's ability to relate to his peers and environment. At the uppermost educational levels—Masters of Arts or Science and Doctors of Philosophy—students are encouraged to add to the total fund of knowledge or opinion within their respective disciplines, to think for themselves, and to assume responsibility for resolving questions having no ready answers.

At all levels, schools play a tremendously important daily role in our socioeconomy. In terms of the far-reaching effects their products, the students, will ultimately have on the course of domestic society and the world, the importance of schools is incalculable. If we are to consider the 8-Day Week at all seriously as an alternative living system, then its effect on schools, students, and scholars must also be considered.

There are approximately 60 million children, adolescents, and university students attending school in the United States. All of them could be affected by the 8-Day Week both directly, as a result of reorganizing school calendars to benefit from this system, and indirectly as a function of their parents' new-found leisure time, which would offer increased opportunity for intrafamily communication of an educational nature.

Some of the scheduling complexities outlined earlier in relation to adult business patterns, such as turning over one-eighth of the work force each day of the 8-day cycle, would appear to be unnecessary and undesirable for schools. Instead, a simple alternating on and off cycle could be employed for two groups, each of which equal roughly half of the total student community, as shown below:

Days of the year	1 2 3 4	5 6 7 8	9 10 11 12	13 14 15 16	17 18 19 20	21 22
Student group	A	B	A	B	A	B

Such an arrangement would appear to lead naturally to the quarter system, which is already gaining in popularity both as a weapon to fight the rampant capital costs faced by school systems everywhere and as a means for students to accelerate their academic progress. A rough comparison between a 4-on, 4-off system of year-round attendance and the classic semester system yields virtual parity in terms of total yearly school days attended:

System	Computation of Days Attended
Semester	40 weeks $\times$ 5 days = 200 minus holidays = 185
4-on, 4-off, 4 quarters	365 divided by 2 = 182½

The above comparison is limited by the fact that it inflexibly hews to a fairly standard semester situation (September through the first week in June) and slavishly adheres to a constant 4-on, 4-off pattern. In fact, far more flexibility already exists in semester-oriented schools, and could be brought into play in connection with 8-day cycling. Some schools, for example, in New York City, operate two shifts per day because of inadequate classroom facilities, and stay open more than 40 weeks to compensate for the shorter daily student hours which stem from double-shifting. Similarly, a 4-on, 4-off quarterly system could be adjusted to meet a variety of needs. For example, students could engage in academic studies for four days and spend all or part of a fifth day engaged in outdoor-oriented activities such as gym, natural science, or field trips. On a year-round basis, students involved in such a system would attend school 200 days per year, including 4 weeks' vacation. Another variation could involve the same 5-day curriculum for three quarters, yielding 174 school days. These fairly obvious examples are given to indicate the tremendous flexibility which lies within a superficially rigid system. Ultimately, it would fall to the school board on the one hand, tempered by students' needs on the other, to determine what approach would be most suitable.

Having laid the basic groundwork as to how organized education systems as we know them could relate to the 8-Day Week, perhaps it would be worth speculating on how such a system might affect young people's learning processes and their school-related lives.

I believe it would offer kids a learning opportunity which can't begin to exist under today's educational system. Currently, the schoolchild is exposed to a curriculum probably comprised of television, his teacher, a building which is usually part of his neighborhood, books and other teaching aids, and a peer group, made up of people having roughly similar backgrounds and attitudes. Added to this assemblage are varying degrees of parental guidance, and the wider environment of a neighborhood, with its potential for observation. This, roughly speaking, is the sum of the average child's present-day learning tools. Involvement in one of the alternative approaches to 8-day cycling should enhance both the qualitative and quantitative aspects of a person's formal learning years. To begin with, class division and alternative cycling will tend to reduce the average number of students present in classrooms on any given day. Aside from offering the opportunity for greater individual attention from teachers as well as enabling the student to participate more fully in the give-and-take of instruction, smaller classes are easier to manage. Thus, less student and teacher time would be wasted on class administration and maintenance of discipline, and more time devoted to getting on with the business at hand. Similarly, smaller classes place less strain on teachers, with the logical result that they can devote more energy to instructing and relating with their pupils than is possible in more strenuous situations involving larger classes. In short, students' strengths and weaknesses can be spotted and dealt with more quickly, noncontributing stress-related situations reduced, and interpersonal student-teacher relationships nurtured. The value of such relationships to the learning process should not be overlooked. It seems fair to say that a student's difficulties with school in general or in a given subject are often traceable to his or her failure to relate to the situation at hand. If teachers are offered greater opportunity to build personal bridges between themselves and their charges, relative gaps will tend to be eliminated and pent-up potential learning capacity will be released.

Among students themselves, in such a classroom situation, a rich opportunity exists for increased communication. Smaller classes are less frightening than larger ones, hence the need to form immediate alliances for social defense purposes would appear to be reduced. The class would have a better chance to exist *as a unit*, as opposed to a collection of groups or cliques. Greater opportunity to examine one's fellows in class would provide a more thoroughly constructed, less superficial basis for relationships *outside the classroom*. In sum, the chance for deeper involvement among students within a classroom situation could encourage better adjusetment to life *in toto*.

Exploration of the 8-Day Week's impact on formal education systems is only a part of the greater question of its effect on the education of youngsters. As was noted earlier, parents either can or do play a major role in the process of building young minds. The extent to which effective parent-child teaching processes take place depends heavily on two factors: (1) the willingness of both parties to communicate, and (2) the opportunity to do so. It would seem fair to speculate, regarding the question of both parties' willingness to develop and continue a dialogue, that the creation of more usable time through rescheduling our lives would lead to greater relaxation among the population at large, hence make us more willing and capable of expressing ourselves and understanding others. The opportunities for greater self-knowledge inherent in The Alternative, as discussed in an earlier chapter, should lead to parents' becoming not only more *willing teachers*, but also more *effective* ones in the sense of being better able to communicate with their children. When one combines the willingness and possibly improved skill for communication with the tremendously increased *opportunity* to do so offered by the 8-Day Week, one reaches the conclusion that current levels of effective parent-child teaching may be improved upon substantially. Such a supposition appears to be reasonable when you recognize the fact that more frequent, *longer* dialogues would be made possible by the availability of greater amounts of usable time to the individuals involved.

Development of a more successful communication between parents and children should lead to a more rapid broadening of the children's perspectives, should encourage greater willingness to learn (among other places, in school), and should generally whet the learner's appetite for further learning experiences.

The final major area in which the 8-Day Week may act to broaden youth is the greatly increased opportunity it offers a child to view and assimilate diverse environments. More usable amounts of time off for parents hold the promise of tremendously increased family mobility. There is a lot to be learned by a child in the course of several days' travel to and from a place he's never been before, or during a series of daily excursions. It seems fair to assume that the more a child sees, the more he or she will assimilate, and the more questions will be asked and answered.

Those who are very fortunate will be those whose families regularly leave town during off cycles and head for a firmly established second environment. These kids will have the chance to view life "in duplicate." They can study and compare city life with whatever alternate they find themselves in as a result of their parents' decision to lead a double life. They will have the chance to develop two sets of friends, two sets of activity patterns, and different sets of interests, as suggested by the differing environments in which they find themselves.

From their earliest days they will be trained to be flexible in their interests and attitudes and highly adaptable to a variety of situations. Such acclimatization would appear to be a precious asset in meeting the constant changes of modern life with equanimity.

Although all the foregoing applies to both primary and secondary school students, major emphasis should probably be placed against the younger group as the reader considers what has been written.

As the student advances scholastically and matures socially, he or she might be expected to benefit in more refined ways from the rearrangement of education systems to relate to the 8-Day Week.

It's probably fair to say that high school students need to spend more time adapting to their personal and social situations than they do actually studying. Adolescence is a period in which people undergo tremendous adjustments in their bodies, emotions, and attitudes. To make the transition from childhood to young adulthood successfully, adolescents must pass through a series of fairly trying experiences. To do so successfully, they need solitude and privacy in substantial quantities on the one hand, and the opportunity to develop a series of relationships with their peers on the other. It seems to me that the current system tends to conflict with needs such as these. It cannot be denied that young people have somehow managed to follow a schedule of school attendance five days out of every seven, do their homework, perform filial duties, and engage in nonsocial extracurricular activities over a period of many generations. They have also succeeded in balancing these requirements with a natural desire to spend time mingling with friends, falling in and out of love, and learning to play the guitar. Still, in doing so, they have probably been forced to compromise one or more of these elements which are natural parts of their lives at this stage. Those who cut down on or virtually relinquish scholastics may find themselves wishing they hadn't done so a few years hence. Those who pay strict attention to their books, and sublimate other adolescent activity to do so, may find themselves socially inadequate in future years. Those who manage to achieve a fine balance of personality, social adjustment, and academic achievement are envied and applauded as being a fairly rare species.

The 8-Day Week should prove conducive to producing higher percentages of such well-balanced individuals, and to the development of relatively better-adjusted, wiser youth in general. This should tend to be so because of the fact that such a system will deliberately encourage nonacademic social progress by making available the time for its development. The conflict which may currently obtain should be substantially reduced by establishing more clear-cut divisions of time allocable to different activities—that is, four days for regimented schooling, four days to grow up at an unregimented rate.

The greater relative freedom that would be offered by The Alternative should encourage teen-agers to find out about life and interpret those findings thoroughly. Social circles would be vastly expanded and the opportunity to build deep relationships with others compounded.

Those teen-agers whose parents regularly commuted to another area during nonworking days would find themselves in the midst of a great learning opportunity. They could, if they wished, develop two separate sets of friends, each of which would probably entertain somewhat different outlooks and engage in somewhat different activities due to distinctions between their environments. Or they could elect to concentrate on one environment for socializing and the other for essentially academic pursuits. They might choose to remain in the city and live with friends and a set, or sets, of surrogate parents, i.e., their friends' parents, or other adults willing to take them in on a regular and extended basis. Such an experience could prove a valuable means of rounding out a young person, whether done in the "city" or in the "country" part of his environment.

Whether their parents were regular commuters or not, teenagers would be able to immerse themselves in nonacademic but nonetheless educational extracurricular pursuits, once the time to do so was made available. Some of us love to read, and will, if possible, plow straight through a book to the detriment of other things which should be attended to, for example, homework. It would seem more pleasant and more productive if avid readers could have four straight days out of every eight to indulge their interest in books. Such would be similarly true of any pursuit which requires time to yield satisfaction—learning to play a musical instrument, mechanics, woodworking, athletics, art, and many others.

For those high schoolers who want or need to hold part-time jobs, the 8-Day Week is ideal. Kids with part-time employment now work before or after school and, frequently, Saturdays. The disadvantages of such a situation are obvious. If, on the other hand, a teen-ager could concentrate his job into two days' work, rather than have it scattered throughout parts of many days, the situation would become easier to bear and manage. Having whole days available for work might also tend to allow entry at an earlier age into jobs that are more interesting, hence more emotionally rewarding, than those currently available to one who must, of necessity, work in fits and starts. A teen-ager who is interested in electronics might stand a better chance of getting a job repairing radios and television sets, rather than, for example, working in a laundromat, if he could be counted on for two full days' work at regular intervals. Since electronic repair is a skill, the pay would probably be better than it is in unskilled jobs. As a result, a teen-ager would not only find the opportunity for more intellectually rewarding work but also need to work fewer hours to earn the same amount of money.

Before moving on to the 8-Day Week's application at the college level, perhaps one additional element of its effect on secondary school students should be pointed out. This element is sports and other extracurricular but school-oriented activities.

Depending on the circumstances within a given school, such as the size of the student body and the attitudes of administrators and coaches, the 8-Day Week could lead to a tremendous increase in the percentage of students who actually get to play varsity sports. In a pure application of the two-shift systems discussed earlier, schools could develop two teams, rather than one, for major sports. It is evident that involvement in athletics helps build character by building people's capacity for the give-and-take which all sports entail. If sports do contribute to the development of balanced personalities, The Alternative would represent a means of roughly doubling the number of people benefited from participation. The stigma which attaches to B-team membership would be lessened or eliminated as talent was spread over teams which resulted from division of talent through classroom scheduling. Weaker athletes would get a chance to improve their skills through more actual playing time than they presently get, while stronger athletes would enjoy a greater opportunity for stardom through reduced competition.

It is probably unrealistic to suppose that coaches would find such a situation palatable. After all, coaches want to win, and probably wouldn't enjoy having to field less than optimum strength, nor to have a coequal rival coach. Such a question, however, is secondary to the importance of equipping teen-agers to lead fruitful, balanced lives in later years. If participation in sports helps build personal balance, then let that be the guiding principle. Questions of chauvinism can be satisfied, if necessary, by holding playoffs at the end of a given sport's season, and fielding the best *combined* team as a unified entry.

Of other extracurricular activities, such as student government or special interest groups, it should suffice to point out that the operation of two schools in one doubles students' chances to participate. Again, the teen-agers' interests appear to be served by increasing their opportunity for nonacademic education.

All in all, a curriculum rearranged to relate to the 8-Day Week appears to offer very exciting possibilities at the secondary school level, from a strictly academic viewpoint as well as that of general education and personality development.

Its application at the university level also would appear to promise greater rewards, to students and faculty members alike, than either can realize under present circumstances.

Nowadays, a college student normally attends either lectures or tutorials sporadically over the span of the 5-day workweek. It is not unusual for a student to find himself enrolled in a variety of courses which meet at 9, 11, and 3 on Mondays, Wednesdays, and Fridays, and at 10, 11, and 2 on Tuesdays and Thursdays. These classes, furthermore, are frequently far distant both from each other and from the student's residence and place of study. The only way a student can relate successfully to such a situation, in terms of regular attendance, is by shuttling on and off campus over and over again. This process makes the student a repetitive short-distance commuter who squanders considerable energy merely coming and going, and tremendous amounts of time between classes—time which, too often, is divided into segments that are too small to be useful for study, use of the library, or any other fruitful activity.

Instead, students consume innumerable cups of coffee, converse, and do parts of crossword puzzles in stints of a half hour, more or less, as they wait throughout the day for their next scheduled class.

The classes themselves, when they are met, are characteristically short, i.e., from forty-five minutes to an hour long. As a result, a student's typical class day may boil down to three hours of class, an hour of walking, two hours wasted during free time, and an hour for lunch. Since university students are frequently expected to read quantities of course-related material and prepare a variety of papers (many requiring hours of library research), they find themselves hard at it after dinner and into the night, making up for the fact that no usable daytime hours were available for sustained study. The net result may be a sufficiently productive but incredibly inefficient 12-to-15-hour day Monday through Thursday, and a barely worthwhile Friday, since Friday evening will more likely be used for socializing than as a time for sustained study.

As things now stand, the student's dilemma promises to continue and enlarge as time passes and campuses grow. Enormous sums of money have been spent and will continue to be spent to add more and more buildings to accommodate tremendous crowds of students from Monday through Friday and to stand silent and empty on weekends. The 8 million-odd post-secondary school students populating our colleges and universities are, in a sense, actively being encouraged to be apathetic, to waste time, to achieve mediocrity—all at enormous expense to themselves, their parents, and taxpayers at large.

A 4-day-on, 4-day-off system of university scheduling would work to reverse the situation as outlined above. Let us consider some of these elements as they might be affected by The Alternative.

To begin with, let us consider the question of "acting"—taking notes or participating in tutorials—versus "thinking," and how these conflicting emotional entities might be better reconciled by cycled scheduling. A student's curriculum can be bunched together within 4 days of an 8-day on and off cycle. Classes can be longer and fewer in number, and the number of useless unscheduled hours between a given student's class meetings reduced. A student who goes to the campus in the morning knowing that he is going to be involved all day in the simple process of "fact gathering"—being lectured to and taking part in seminars and tutorial discussions—can leave the need for quiet introspection at home. He need not suffer as much lethargy as he has grown accustomed to after too many time-killing cups of coffee at the student union. He will be environmentally allowed, and even encouraged, to become highly involved, hence more substantially instructed, in a subject when he is exposed at greater length to the topic at hand. A 2-hour class is often more interesting than one half that long, assuming the subject matter and the teacher both have merit in the student's eyes.

A day on campus will become a fuller one, hence more of a potential reward in itself. It will become a more clearly defined, purposeful experience. It will become more valuable as a learning opportunity and as time spent in a student's life.

The reverse is also true. Those 4 days during which the student would not be attending classes would represent a tremendous opportunity for those who would be scholarly, more than sufficient time to do one's outside reading for those having normal scholastic interest, and an excellent social opportunity for all.

The allocation of 4 days out of 8 to individual reading and research could develop our universities into tremendously productive institutions compared with what they can currently achieve in terms of educating their students. American colleges and universities might be described as offering intensive instruction and less intensive reading as a means to instilling an education among the student body. European universities might be said to offer limited instruction and intensive reading to achieve the same end. A system involving 4/4 cycling could yield the best of both systems—that is, an education grounded on *both* intensive instruction and the development of a greater student capacity for self-instruction. Through expanded opportunity to read, to delve into a subject, to lead himself to knowledge, the student might gain not only an education but also more of the tools of self-reliance, which can be helpful in later life.

Those who teach at the university level could also benefit from a 4-day-on, 4-day-off cycling system, both as scholars and as instructors. Today's professor tends to be torn between the desires to be helpful to his students and to enhance his position within his chosen field. These desires are substantially antithetical since they both contend for the professor's time during the workweek. If an instructor is to teach his students, he must make efforts to ensure that his lecture notes, required texts, and recommended reading material are up to date, representative, and relevant not only to the subject per se but also to the available body of knowledge in the subject's parent field and to a changing world. A good example of how much work such a process can require may lie in a course such as basic American history. If a professor is to stay up to date even in such a broad survey course, he must, among other things, take note of and include findings generated by specialists in black studies, who have unleashed a torrent of information since this relatively new discipline came into being. He should be able to include American Indian studies and the work of foreign historians as it becomes available and relates to this country's own progress. Failure to do so will tend to make such a professor a poor teacher to his students, who depend fairly heavily upon him for guidance and elucidation. Another area of "instruction" which professors currently choose or may be forced to short-change is that of office hours, during which they are, or should be, available to students who desire personal contact regarding a course.

One reason why professors may be regularly unavailable for student contact is that they frequently feel obliged to consult to private industry or to publish learned tracts and articles as a means of maintaining their economic or professional status. A great deal of time and effort is required to perform such activities at a high level of competence. Thus, the professor who publishes or consults faces the same type of problem as his students—that of trying to use bits and pieces of time sandwiched in between his lectures and seminars to pursue his other work. As things now stand, it is fair to presume that the ambitious professor's work load spills over into nights and weekends. The establishment of a larger, well-defined period of time for other pursuits would help clarify such a person's situation from the standpoints of planning and executing his extracurricular activity. Since the companies for which he might consult would be open 7 days a week, present-day conflicts regarding weekdays and weekends would tend to be resolved. Consultations could be scheduled around the professor's free time more easily than can be done now. His class days would become more consolidated, too, so that 4 fairly well organized days out of 8 could be more fully employed in the business of teaching and meeting with students. The other days would represent a windfall of consolidated opportunity to conduct research or consult at will, as well as providing time for leisure. The point here is not that an active, ambitious, and conscientious professor would work less, but rather that he would be able to put his available time to more productive use than the system now permits.

A system involving two identical class cycles at all levels of schooling implicitly carries with it the inference that the number of employed teachers would double. Fortunately, this country is well equipped with teachers or individuals qualified to teach. According to the *Wall Street Journal,* 37 percent of all college graduates are "certified to teach." Others who have graduated in the past and are qualified to teach may have taken other jobs due to the tightness of the "teaching market," which finds itself with a superabundance of applicants for nonexistent positions. In the change to 4/4 school cycling, then, there would apparently be no insoluble "teaching gap" due to lack of qualified talent within the country. According to *Business Week*, the number of superfluous teachers could reach nearly 2 million by 1980, representing unemployment of all types of instructors ranging from kindergarten teachers to would-be college professors who hold Ph.Ds.

Within an over-all education budget estimated at $80 billion per year by *Time* magazine, it might be possible to pay these additional teachers' salaries. It might not only be possible, but might even *lead to a reduction in the over-all cost of "education"* by obviating the need for massive school construction as a result of making double use of the facilities already at hand.

It should be obvious that money spent on teachers to teach in an improved (i.e., smaller) classroom atmosphere, in a rhythm conducive to vitality and enthusiasm among students and teachers alike, is better spent than money devoted to the construction of more and more classrooms. If this be so, adoption of a 4/4 cycled schooling schedule could lead to a revolution in this country's educational system from all points of view. The most important viewpoint, however, is that of:

> 31,500,000 elementary school students;
> 20,100,000 high school students;
> 7,600,000 university students.

They are not only the future of this country, but represent to a significant degree the future of the world.

7 The 8-Day Reformation

■

Potential Effects on Our Relationship with Life
as a Whole, Including Money, Friendship,
Community, and Growing Old

The 8-Day Week is a natural, if gigantic, step in consumerism. Although it is an entirely populist concept in terms of its tendency to restore significant losses in personal freedom, it promises to solve communal problems which persist and fester despite the best efforts to the contrary of administrators at all levels of government. That is, perhaps, its unique and special beauty. Most systems tend to put pressure on individuals in order to lessen the collective load, or to do the reverse, i.e., place a burden on the "system" to lighten the individual onus. Our present living context attempted to do the latter over a period of time, but has reached the point where *both systems and individuals are overstrained*. All the money we can print, all the GNP increases we can generate simply won't cover the cost of meeting our urban needs as they are currently organized. In going to a populist, consumerist system, we would be not only restoring a considerable amount of personal freedom, but also making better use of human beings as potential assets. On the other hand, the human burden (or social overhead) which has been placed on governments through a combination of urban crowding and spiraling costs will be lessened and become more manageable. The long trend toward urban and human neglect and decay will be arrested at last, and a basis for urban reconstruction and rejuvenation will have been established.

These promises of urban improvement and the restoration of humanity to our lives are general, if tremendous, values inherent in the 8-Day Week. The underpinnings of this generality are also interesting and valuable to us, both as individuals and as members of society.

The 8-Day Week offers the possibility of a fundamental Reformation, not simply in the way it would affect our work, or education, but also in how it might alter our attitudes toward life as a whole. Such a Reformation can be exemplified in a variety of ways.

First, it offers the opportunity to refocus our lives in terms of primary, secondary, and tertiary activities in which we normally find ourselves engaged. Today, we focus more time and attention on our jobs than we do on other activities. The fact that we spend most of 5 days out of every 7 commuting and working makes it so. Thus, whether we want them to or not, our jobs take the greater part of the time and energy available to us. It might be fair to describe this set of circumstances as an involuntary, or unconscious, assignment of priority. The system controls our lives, while we ourselves tend to follow along.

The 8-Day Week would tend to counter such a "built-in" imbalance between the time allotted to work, contrasted with time available for other pursuits, by establishing an equal number of days for work and leisure respectively. Once such a mechanism has been established, it clearly follows that working people will no longer have a "decision" regarding priorities forced on them. Instead, they themselves will have a decision to make. They will, for the first time, have the freedom to decide *consciously* how a major portion of their lives is to be spent. It could be speculated that the simple fact of being in a position to make such a decision could have a significant impact on the thought processes and attitudes of the 80 million people involved in such a transition.

The emergence of more free time away from work may, among

other things, lead people to consider their occupations more objectively than heretofore because of the placement, in a sense, of more distance between themselves and their sources of income. Should such a process take place, a variety of outcomes might result. For example, people might:

1. Find their jobs to be a home and refuge, enjoy them more, thus work harder and more effectively. (Such seems to be the experience of Group Health, Inc., with a test of a version of the 4-day week, partly reported in the *New York Times* as follows: "There's been a change in general attitude in this shop," Dr. Melcher said. "A year ago, there seemed to be more discontented people. You don't see that now.")

2. Discover their jobs are unsuitable to either their financial or emotional needs, then deliberately choose and gather qualifications for other employment.

3. Become detached from their work, neither loving nor hating it, but treating it as a source of money having sparse emotional overtones.

An even more obvious consideration might be that of what to do with ourselves when not at work. If people in great numbers find consuming outlets for emotions and energy outside the confines of their employment, a broad-scale reordering of priorities will have taken place. The job will have been displaced as the center of attention for a significant population within the total of society, having been replaced by an array of other foci. Such a change in focus and attitude could have a tremendous "ripple effect" on the economy, on politics, social attitudes, child-rearing, religion—in other words, on the mores of our society.

An element as basic as our attitude toward money, standard of living, or life style might change radically as part of a Reformation inspired by the 8-Day Week. Under present circumstances, it could be said that money is time. People who have a great deal of money can always stop working, if they wish, and enjoy the leisure *that their money can buy*. The luxury of time in abundance is the preserve of the wealthy, not available to those of us who have to work for a living. If, however, the workweek is rearranged so as to give everybody half the year off, this money-related distinction between the wealthy and the not-so-wealthy will tend to be diminished. In the process, the importance of money itself *as a means to achieving leisure* might also be expected to diminish. The energy now being expended by many individuals in pursuit of money might be redirected to other, more human goals, such as "the pursuit of happiness."

On the other hand, money might become more important, or maintain its status relative to other values, with the onset of the 8-Day Week. Such could be the case if increased leisure were to lead to increased consumption of goods and services by the average family, because of the increase in leisure itself.

I tend to think that a balance would be struck between the two attitudes which could conceivably emerge toward money, and suspect that, overall, the importance of money per se would tend to diminish in harmony with a diminished relationship between money and an improved life style. Such a suspicion would appear reasonable in light of the fact that the basic thesis of the 8-Day Week is one of *getting more out of life for your effort (money),* thus making the accumulation of more dollars relatively less necessary in terms of either survival or maintaining a certain living standard. This would appear true of dollars "indirectly spent" through taxes on highways, bridges, schools, etc., as well as those directly spent by individuals for goods and services. In short, as the effectiveness of each dollar spent *increased,* the need to accumulate dollars indiscriminately would *decrease*.

It could also be speculated that people's life styles would undergo major adjustments as an extension of a change in attitude toward job, money, self, and family. As the equation between success and money became less valid in people's minds, the artifacts which denote success in our society might become less sought after. Striving for a bigger house, a newer car, or another color television set might lessen in favor of enjoying oneself and one's surroundings. Comfortable clothes might become more important than making sure one owned the "correct" outfits.

Currently, a person may make efforts to keep his house in good repair, and a sharp eye on his neighbors' homes, in order to prevent a loss in the value of his own real estate investment. Though his efforts tend to have the desired effect, the motives underlying them may be basically selfish and defensive. Given more leisure to develop a greater sense of self, such an individual conceivably could find himself with more self to give, namely, an improved communal awareness. Such an awareness could be expressed, among other ways, as a desire to make his community a better place to live for all its inhabitants. The growth of community spirit in place of boosterism could be expected to yield not only the same value-protecting effects as boosterism would, but also even greater dividends to the population as this spirit pervaded. Principal among these could be renewed feelings of pride and fellowship, which currently appear to be systematically declining.

On a personal basis, the concept of friendship could accede to a higher level as we became better equipped to befriend others and had more leisure to evaluate people as potential friends. Over time we might replace social sets—*groups of people* with whom we regularly associate—with an *accumulation of individuals* whom we have come to know, enjoy, and respect, and whose company we value for the positive reinforcement it brings to us when we come in contact.

These days, many of us drink too much. We use alcohol as a release from pressure. Its depressant effects help us wind down tensions which we normally accumulate in the course of facing pressures which have become a part of normal urban existence. We use it as a refuge, that is, drink defensively for various reasons ranging from shutting out unpleasantness to giving us the courage to be sociable at cocktail parties. The Reformation might lead to a reduction in our dependency on alcohol as a crutch. If the pressures associated with work were lessened, the need to counteract such pressures might also decline proportionately. As our relationships with ourselves, our families, and our friends became deeper and more relaxed, our need for artificial help in participating in them should be decreased.

Among normal people, the reduced intake of alcohol should lead to better health in the physical sense, since our bodies would be required to process less of an element that is noxious to humans. A reduced psychological dependence on alcohol would indicate better mental health as well, as manifested by a reduced drinking-related neurosis. Substitute personalities, based substantially on alcohol, would appear to be less desirable than genuine ones growing out of self.

Another major social group would be affected. Our society, as constructed, tends to discard older people before they are dead. As our people approach the fullness of time, they are actively encouraged to feel and to be useless, encouraged to believe that their value to society from a certain point in time onward will be nil. They are made to feel dependent on a combination of elements, e.g., company retirement benefits, Social Security, their depletable savings, and relatives.

The *New York Daily News* carried a series of articles on retirement and the effects, under present circumstances, which such new status can have on those involved, saying in part:

> More than 1.5 million Americans retire from work each year, many with the hope that with the end of the long grind of work will come a rejuvenation, a kind of rebirth. For a significant number of them—and the number, like the number who retire, is growing—retirement is as much a shock as birth. It can be the first time in their lives that they have been on their own.
>
> Marvin Veronee, associate director of retirement studies at the University of Chicago, says that, "The patterns of our society are such

that people go through periods of dependence—dependence on their families, on educational institutions and on the organizations they work for.

"Finally, as they face the last quarter of their lives, they retire and for the first time have to go at life alone.

. . . "A lot of people think money equals successful retirement, and that executives have no problems. Many times we find that that's not true, that the executive may have lost a high status without which he cannot function."

The progress toward a feeling of uselessness and dependency is easy to trace. The route is defined by the big company where, as likely as not, a person for whom retirement is in the offing is employed. From the point where a man or woman become too old to change from Company A to Company B (because Company B doesn't want an older employee), he or she becomes dependent on the employer. Between the ages of 45 to 50 and retirement, such a person must bend every effort to keep his job. To lose it is to court disaster. In this knowledge, the older employee strives to do nothing untoward, nothing to attract attention, nothing exceptional, nothing to rock the big-company boat. He tries to become an invisible man. By doing so, he becomes one of the least productive elements within a given company. The firm knows it and encourages further efforts toward achieving invisibility on his part by looking past him to younger, more vital men who still dare to risk their security in a calculated gamble to reach greater corporate heights. The older employee, therefore, actually achieves uselessness well before his true ability to contribute has been extinguished. As a result, he actively trains for the day he is "officially" declared worthless, through the act of being retired, long before the moment itself arrives.

Despite the fact that such individuals go through a process of devaluation in terms of their company's society's, and their own opinions of themselves as contributors, they are, at the same time, *made to pretend otherwise.* They, too, must devote the major portion of their waking hours to going through the motions of working and commuting. They must suffer the strains associated with job-holding in an atmosphere of almost total anonymity and self-degradation. The 2-day weekend offers little opportunity for them to rediscover and regenerate themselves, even though the need to do so is more urgent for such people than it is for those who are younger and more likely to believe in their own personal worth.

After such years of conditioning, the retiree is relatively unable to fend for himself, poorly equipped to fill the tremendous number of void hours facing him between the time of retirement and total incapacity or death. In a classic situation—one involving a for-merly employed man and a wife whose life has been devoted to homemaking—there lurks the potential for further trouble in the form of misunderstanding, conflict in interests, and their respec-tive approaches to filling the hours which constitute a lifetime. Whereas the man's pattern of time allocation has been essentially eliminated due to his loss of employment, the woman has long since created a daily pattern for spending her time, having been retired at least since their youngest child left home. The man "gets under-foot." Any attempt to run the house as he ran his office is likely to meet resistance from entrenched management in the person of his wife, who has handled domestic affairs perfectly well for many years prior.

This long, sad, and true scenario need not necessarily be. If a man were able to devote half of his working years to discovering himself, developing new interests, building new friendships, and working out a satisfactory symbiosis with his wife, the approach to retirement, retirement itself, and its aftermath would not be the disheartening experiences they now must be.

The division of time between job and leisure would provide years of training for the moment when one is set free from society. During those years, the "retirement trainee" would not only have the opportunity to develop alternative outlets for his energy and creativity, but also, in the act of living more of his own life, *tend to maintain higher levels of vigor, self-respect, and productivity at work.* The act of discovering who he is and what he can do should diminish the paralysis which is currently encouraged through fear of the uncertain retirement years, and fear of being forced into early retirement through discharge.

Older people could be happier, more productive parts of a whole society to which they can continue to contribute, after having passed through a transition in which their personalities were sustained and encouraged to grow, rather than brutally canceled.

The current system of work and leisure has smothered us as human beings at all levels of age, education, and occupation, to the point where an urgent need for relief from this process has been reached. The 8-Day Week offers potential release from such stultification, while offering new opportunities for significant human benefits.

8 Problems and Questions

■

*Simultaneous Cycling for Married Couples;
Idleness Is the Devil's Workshop; Keep Holy
the Sabbath; Small-Business Survival; A Setback for
Urban Construction; It's Illegal; Unpredictable
Union Attitudes*

A system as radical as the 8-Day Week can neither be proposed nor be brought into being without considering the difficulties
that its adoption would evoke. There are tremendous barriers
standing in the way of its acceptance. Some of these obstacles are
very real. For example, the problem of maintaining coincidental
schedules for married couples is a major one. Certain laws must be
changed if the 8-Day Week is to become legal, much less practical.

On the other hand, there are customs which militate against its
acceptance, and superstitions held by certain people regarding their
fellow-men which will prejudice them against such a radical change.
Since this book is intended as a blueprint for reform, such problems
and questions must be dealt with as fairly and openly as possible.

It is clear that, were an 8-Day Week adopted, a major adjustment would have to be made by almost everybody between the
ages of 6 and 65. An entirely new rhythm of living is called for
during working and leisure hours. Although The Alternative offers
4 days off out of every 8 and a 35-hour week when computed on
a year-round basis, it also calls for a 10-hour work schedule during
those 4 days when we work.

There is no denying that a 10-hour day is a hard one, especially
for a working housewife who may have a husband to feed and

children to care for in addition to work-related responsibilities. She will have to overcome the problems associated with child care for an hour or two more than she must currently make provision for. Both adults may (or may not) be more tired than they now are at the end of an average workday. Unless people can learn to improve their logistical skills—become better planners of their trips to the supermarket and better long-range organizers of their lives in general—the 8-Day Week will create end-of-the-day strains which could result in physical weariness and short tempers.

On the other hand, people are already putting in something resembling a 50-hour 5-day week, when commuting is taken into consideration, and must necessarily make the kinds of logistic provisions described above if they are to have any time whatsoever to themselves after they have met the requirements of their employment and household maintenance.

It would seem fair to say, then, that perhaps the major individual adjustment required in adapting to the 8-Day Week is a mental one involving inspection of the custom of working 5 days a week and determining whether or not this custom has outlasted its relevance to our lives. In this connection it should be repeated that in 1929, only 5 percent of the working population was on a 5-day week. The remaining 95 percent were accustomed to working either all or part of Saturday. In fact, the 5-day week did not become the norm until after the end of World War II. When the 5-day week became a common reality, working people had no trouble adapting to it.

Experiments with other forms of a shorter workweek indicate that given more leisure time on the one hand and a longer workday on the other, the people involved both find that adjustments need be made and succeed in making these adjustments without undue strain. Fortunately, society is becoming ever more able to adapt quickly to change as it presents itself in a variety of forms. Such basic adaptability should stand us all in good stead in meeting the challenge offered by The Alternative.

A technical problem of monumental proportions exists, however, in another area of special importance to married couples when both husband and wife are working. This is the problem of synchronized scheduling. Remembering that the scheduling recommended here calls for changing roughly one-eighth of the total work force on each of the days within the 8-day cycle, it becomes clear that the odds are 7 to 1 against any two people's being on *identical* cycles.

It is obvious that such people *cannot be scheduled randomly* by their respective employers. To do so would be to invite unhappiness and a labor revolt on an unprecedented scale. It is equally obvious, then, that a great deal of flexibility will be required of employers as they attempt to match their corporate needs with the needs of their employees. Company A, which may employ a husband, will have to relate to Company B, which employs this man's wife. When you bear in mind that roughly 18 million working women in this country are married, the size of this problem becomes apparent. A tremendous number of adjustments and readjustments would necessarily have to be made in order to resolve *the scheduling problems* of working couples as well as *the operational problems* which adjusting these same people's schedules would create for their employers. Fortunately, we are familiar with computer programming technology and have available considerable computer capacity. If companies cooperate among themselves, employing pool computers to relate their respective personnel needs to the facts of their respective employees—i.e., who is married to whom—such complicated problems can be solved. Similarly, areas of conflict between companies should surface rapidly, providing at least the opportunity for discussion and resolution of their differences through negotiation, concession, and compromise.

The most helpful element in solving this problem is the fact that there is no such thing as a desirable or undesirable schedule within 8-day cycling. All schedules are equal. No one can "reserve" weekends in the sense of always being off Saturdays and Sundays since the present weekend is irrelevant to the 8-Day Week. Thus, whatever cycle group a married couple might find itself within will matter less than the fact of their being in it together.

This problem of unified scheduling for married people is the largest one I can find. Difficult as it would be to solve, it seems to me that it *can* be solved if a serious effort is made by those concerned. It is comforting to believe that the monumental logistics involved would have social validity.

A related question is that of friends: how their cycles would relate to our own, and how this relationship might affect our ability to socialize. The answer is that the odds are 7 to 1 in favor of you and your friends' having one or more days off in common within every 8-day period. The odds are 50–50 that you will have two or more days off and on in common with friends. Inspection of the boxed-in portion of the following chart demonstrates this. Simply assign yourself mentally to any one of the cycle groups, then look up and down vertically on the chart; leisure days for your cycle group occur during those days when your cycle group is not shown:

Date

1	2	3	4	5	6	7	8	9	10	11	12	13	14	15	16	17	18

Day of the week

M	T	W	Th	F	Sa	Su	M	T	W	Th	F	Sa	Su	M	T	W	Th

A			B			A			B			A
	C			D			C			D		C
		E			F			E			F	
		G			H			G			H	

Since the odds favor our ability to socialize, and since the 8-Day Week offers more time to attend to the responsibilities which attach to housekeeping and homemaking, it could well be that we would be able to spend more time with friends, even if we worked on somewhat differing schedules, than we can under a system where we have identical schedules for work and leisure.

It is conceivable that questions might be raised regarding certain social side effects that might result from people's having half the year off from work. Specifically, what would people do with all that time, and would its availability lead to a rise in crime and other antisocial activity, thereby encouraging a trend toward cultural decay?

This kind of question has been voiced consistently as an argument against improved working schedules whenever labor has striven for a shorter workweek. It seems fairly natural that such a question might be posed by members of a culture which had a strictly established and accepted work ethic at its roots, and who may still be more inclined to cling to "moral" tenets than relate to an evolving situation. Idleness is not necessarily the devil's workshop any more than relentless "constructive" activity is an unmixed good, either for the individual or for society.

To my knowledge there is no available evidence that crime or other antisocial activities increase as a result of increases in leisure time among the general population. It would seem more logical and natural to speculate that the chance for greater relaxation and self-realization would work in the opposite direction. The notion that the tensions and stress of present-day urban life exacerbate neurotic or antisocial tendencies is broadly accepted.

In addition to the logic of the above argument, there is some available evidence that the average adult will put whatever additional free time placed at his disposal to constructive use. A small group of workers (over 100) completed a questionnaire designed to determine what they did with their additional free time when their employer changed from a normal 5-day workweek to one in which they worked 4 days and enjoyed a 3-day weekend. The base in this study is small—hence not statistically projectable. Nonetheless, the increases in a variety of leisure-time activities cited by respondents to the questionnaire may be considered for their directional value. A 319 percent increase in swimming and boating led the pack, closely followed by resting, relaxing and loafing, which were up 269 percent. Indulgence in travel, visiting relatives, otherwise unidentified hobbies, and movie, concert, and theater attendance all showed increases exceeding 100 percent. As did reading. Activities directly related to the home (working around the house or spending time with one's family) did not increase dramatically, the reason being that these two were apparently treated as prime responsibilities in a 5-on, 2-off weekly regimen. In other words, the great majority of respondents *already* devoted attention to such domestic duties, so large percentage increases in these response categories were not possible.

In discussing the concept of the 8-Day Week with a wide variety of people, I have frequently been asked a question regarding its impact on religion, religious institutions, and religious people. Usually, the question has been phrased like this: "I'm not particularly religious myself, but do you think that people in the Bible Belt, or those who *are* religious, could bring themselves to work in good conscience on Sundays?" In fact, this question has been raised more frequently than any other in conversations about the 8-Day Week.

The answer to this question can be found through interpretation of the Third Commandment, which explicitly directs that the Sabbath be kept holy. Those who strictly obey this Commandment do not work on Saturday, or Sunday, depending upon their religion, giving instead that day to God. The result is that 52 such days per year are God's days. There are, in other words, a number of days assigned to homage *on a regular basis* to a greater being. The word "Sabbath" itself reinforces *the concept of regularity,* since it means the seventh day of the week. I can only hope and speculate that religious leaders and the laity in their flocks could find a means of requiring regular observance of a "God's day." Perhaps it could be every sixth day, perhaps every eighth, related to a given communicant's work cycle, rather than related to the calendar. It would seem that *the idea of regular worship* is more basic to the Third Commandment than the day (or days) which has been observed historically for that purpose. If I am mistaken, if religious leaders cannot be flexible on this point, then a certain amount of disruption of the 8-Day Week would result. The extent of such disruption can only be measured after the fact, however, due to the unpredictability of man's conscience.

On the other hand, if a majority of religious leaders were to agree with the concept of *regular worship,* rather than worship *on Sunday* (or Saturday) only, it would seem fair to conclude that church attendance, and participation in church-related activities by the faithful, would increase sharply. The 8-Day Week would give to those who wished it a tremendously increased opportunity to live a religious life.

Still another problem lies in the area of small business enterprises. Companies and partnerships employing only a small number of people do not have the "organizational momentum" of large ones. A law firm comprising two partners and a secretary does not possess sufficient employees to straddle a business calendar that stretches from one end of the year to the other without remit. Neither does a small delicatessen, most laundries and dry cleaners, or private medical practices. Such situations, which may account for between 2 and 5 percent of the total work force, would probably have to make significant adjustments either in their staffs or in the way they do business. Perhaps several illustrations of the problems small companies might encounter and how they could relate to (and sometimes profit from) them would be useful here.

The two partners in a law firm mentioned above, having a secretary as their sole employee, cannot function along the classic lines laid out for the 8-Day Week. Instead, they would have to adopt an alternative system of their own which related to restructured court sessions and business calendars. Their role would be similar to that of members of upper management in larger companies, who already schedule their own hours. Depending on their circumstances, these partners could relate to their situation in a number of ways. If, for example, each partner had clients who were more or less exclusively his own business, rather than business handled by both partners as a team, then each partner would be required to schedule his working life around his clients' needs. Such scheduling would probably be erratic, ranging from day-to-day alternation of work and rest to, possibly, fairly long uninterrupted spates of either activity or leisure. If, on the other hand, these same lawyers preferred to handle all their business in common, they would probably adopt a scheduling system which allowed for discussion among themselves of the status of various cases with which they were involved. One way this could be accomplished is through adoption of an 8-day cycle containing 5 workdays and 3 leisure days for each partner. Were the partners to elect to do this, they would be able to meet and/or work in common every fourth day, as the following chart demonstrates:

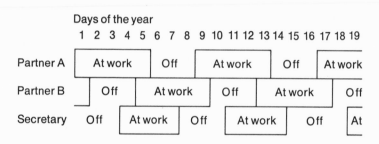

It can be seen from this example that the two partners are paying the price of entrepreneurship, that is, working longer hours and days than they would have to if employed by a large firm able to meet the exigencies of practicing law with greater manpower, hence also able to establish a classic 8-Day Week. On the other hand, it should also be noted in the above that the partners' secretary, *who presumably is not an entrepreneuse*, is able to enjoy a cycle of 4 days at work and 4 days off, while helping both partners and providing a "bridge" between them. The firm in question might also merge with another partnership, and avoid altogether the problems posed in this example.

Certain other types of small business would also have to make significant adjustments in relating to the proposed new workweek, while benefiting substantially from it. In every urban area there are luncheonettes, delicatessens, and restaurants which are entirely dependent upon the presence of business for their livelihood in the form of a lunch-hour trade. Such establishments, located in business centers having essentially no resident populations (for example, in the Wall Street area), now do a tremendous volume around the noon hour Mondays through Fridays, and are closed weekends. In fact, most such establishments are forced to *turn away business* daily because of their limited capacities. They are, in other words, a classic example of what happens when capacity is overloaded at certain times and underused at others.

Expansion of the workweek to include all 7 days of the traditional week would cause a problem for such businesses by creating the need for more employees, including another manager. By way of compensation for the problems inherent in expanding a given work force, however, would be a potential increase in gross income ranging upward to 40 percent above current levels.

Another, generally much larger type of enterprise would probably encounter quite a different situation. In city after city, an unabated construction boom has been taking place. This construction has been a reflection of the need for more and better offices and homes for business and urban residents. Although more will be said on this subject later, it should be pointed out at this stage that the 8-Day Week implicitly calls for the use of *less office space*, and possibly less urban living space, than is currently being demanded. Such reduced demand would stem from potentially *greater use* of leasehold office space by employers and, concomitantly, *a reduction in total square footage* needed to accommodate employees on any given business day. Although all companies have people in their employ who are considered to be sufficiently important to warrant the reservation of certain office space for their exclusive use, they also normally employ many more people who are not considered to be unique or special in the sense of their requiring working space exclusively reserved for their use. Whenever such "secondary" employees can be caused to "share" working space by working on alternating cycles, the employer will benefit in the form of a reduction in the amount of space which he must lease, thus contributing to a reduction in demand for industrial real estate.

A 10 percent reduction in demand for urban real estate would obviously have a significant impact on companies which construct, own, and manage buildings. The 8-Day Week could conceivably result in a 30 to 40 percent reduction in demand for office space as firms and individuals applied the concept of *getting more for less* to their leaseholds. Obviously, construction companies and lessors would have to respond intelligently to such a dramatic change in circumstances. Their response would probably take the form of drastically reduced urban construction and substantially improved services and maintenance in already completed buildings as a means of remaining competitive. The least attractive leaseholds available would probably become vacant in time, and subject to demolition or considerable renovation.

It is possible that the firms owning marginal buildings which are unfit for renovation could find a means of contributing the sites on which they stood to the cities where they are located, to become parks or playgrounds. The firms donating such buildings might possibly be compensated for the gesture by tax write-offs. The cities themselves might find the funds to create and maintain such parks within their existing budgets, a portion of which could be reallocated from urban construction (for which demand would be lessened as pressure on urban facilities lessened) to the maintenance of already existing facilities.

Despite such accommodations as this, it cannot be denied that the 8-Day Week would negatively affect urban real estate developers and owners, who have, until now, been bending efforts toward meeting continued demand for increased office space. It is to be hoped that such firms can find other outlets for their capital, rather than be trapped by their own failure to relate to changes in demand.

A final problem lies in the area of labor legislation and, possibly, the attitudes of organized labor. Two national laws, the Walsh-Healey Public Contracts Act and the Contract Work Hours and Safety Standards Acts, call for payment to workers at the rate of time-and-a-half, rather than normal pay rates, for any time over 8 hours spent on the job during any given day, regardless of the total working hours put in by an employee over the course of a given workweek. This legislation applies to employees engaged in fulfilling government contracts. Such employees number between 3.5 and 4 million workers, or less than 5 percent of the total work force. Some attempt has been made by companies interested in a 4-day 40-hour workweek and a 3-day weekend to obtain waivers of this overtime pay requirement in order to keep down the cost of offering their employees greater leisure time. Such attempts at obtaining waivers of this sort have tended to be nullified by organized labor organizations. Obviously, any legislation which calls for overtime pay after 8 hours' work would apply equally to the 8-Day Week as it now does to working days within a 7-day period, since it relates to a single day without regard for that day's context.

There are also assorted state labor laws on the books which variously forbid employers to require *female* employees to work more than 8 hours a day, or prescribe overtime pay rates for such work. Luckily, the trend toward feminism and equal rights for women has carried with it a tendency for states to repeal sexist labor legislation. In 1963, forty states plus the District of Columbia carried laws specifically restricting working hours for women along the lines just described. The passage of Title VII of the Civil Rights Act of 1964 has carried repeal of these laws at the state level in its wake. There now appear to be only twelve states where such laws have not either been done away with or substantially revised to treat labor equally, regardless of sex. Several states allow for waivers, after application through proper channels, from such restrictive legislation based on sex lines.

Still, there remains a problem in the form of state legislation which, one way or another, would tend to bar four 10-hour workdays out of seven and, presumably would also bar four 10-hour workdays out of eight. The February 1972 *Conference Board Record* lists these problem states as follows:

Arkansas	New Mexico
California	North Carolina
Connecticut	North Dakota
District of Columbia	Ohio
Illinois	Oklahoma
Kansas	Rhode Island
Louisiana	South Carolina
Maine	Texas
Massachusetts	Utah
Missouri	Virginia
Nevada	Washington

The 8-Day Week cannot become a reality until state laws make such an approach economic for employers. The fact that the 8-Day Week works out, over a year's time, to be a 35-hour average workweek—a 12½ percent reduction in time when compared to current work hours—should encourage legislators to adjust the laws as necessary to accommodate this system.

Organized labor, however, might not see it exactly that way. There is ample evidence that unions do not wish to accommodate employers in their attempts to adopt, or experiment with, a 3-day weekend and a 4-day 40-hour workweek. Unions fought long and, at times, bitterly with management to win the 8-hour day. They view four 10-hour days out of every seven as a step backward, and have even gone so far as to nullify "no overtime" agreements reached by locals at the national level. Unions would apparently prefer to see their members working a 32-hour week—four 8-hour days out of every seven. Their response to the 8-Day Week may differ from their response to a situation involving 3-day weekends. The extra day off promised by The Alternative, the per-hour raise implicit in its shorter hours, and the improved quality of life it promises could prove to be a sufficient inducement. Perhaps it would be suitable to quote Leonard Woodcock, president of the United Auto Workers, from *Forbes* magazine:

> The solution may be, particularly if we have the chronic unemployment we seem to, to shorten the workweek, but use the plant all week round. I can see one crew working four days and another working three, including Saturday and Sunday, but the second might get paid as much as the first because they've got those two undesirable days.

A negative attitude on organized labor's part toward the 8-Day Week could constitute a real problem, especially as organized labor is in a position to affect labor legislation. A positive attitude toward this system among members of organized labor could have a great effect in terms of altering existing legislation to accommodate it.

It might be worth pointing out and bearing in mind that powerful as it is, organized labor *is not all labor*. In fact, roughly, 1 out of every 5 employed people belongs to a union. Put another way, 4 out of 5 people who work for a living *do not belong to a union*.

If 80 percent of the working population finds itself agreeable to a better life, and if their employers find the 8-Day Week affordable, then a resisting 20 percent will find itself fighting a rear-guard action, rather than being in the vanguard, where unions have customarily been on questions of working conditions.

9 Alternatives to the 8-Day Week

■

The 4-On, 3-Off Week; The 3-On, 4-Off Week;
The 7-On, 7-Off Week; Staggered Hours;
And Why They Won't Work

Great interest has been shown recently in alternatives to the 5-day workweek by members of management at a variety of companies and by the working people in their employ. Management's motive in either exploring or adopting an alternative to the present norm can be found in a variety of desires, two of which can be fairly said to be universal, and a third of which may have occasionally come into play as revised work schedules were considered. The two leading motives, which I believe to have been relatively constant, could be described as follows:

1. The wish to give employees a better life by rearranging work and leisure time to make the latter more usable, and
2. The wish to attract an effective, productive, loyal work force and to reduce tardiness and absenteeism by offering desirable working conditions.

The third motive is the desire to increase profits through greater use of assets, such as equipment capital.

Other than the 8-Day Week, there are four alternatives to the 5-day week that appear to warrant discussion as background in considering the merits of the 8-Day Week itself. Of these, the most significant is the 4-day week. The 4-day week is a vertical extension of the trend toward fewer workdays within a 7-day period. In its purest form, it calls for four 10-hour workdays, usually Monday through Thursday, and a 3-day weekend. This system, which rearranges a week into more usable blocks of time, has attracted considerable attention and interest. In fact, a book, *4 Days, 40 Hours*, was published on the subject in 1970. This book represents a compilation of results obtained by thirty-odd companies with a 4/3 week. Between the time of its publication and late 1972, the number of companies which either had adopted or were experimenting with a 4/3 week had grown from the initial handful covered in *4 Days, 40 Hours* to approximately 2,000, with a combined employment roll of perhaps 200,000 workers—approximately one-quarter of one percent of the total work force.

This system, along with the others described briefly below, will be analyzed in some detail later in this chapter in comparison with the 8-Day Week.

The second alternative, which has attracted some interest and very limited use, is a 3-day, 12-hour-a-day workweek, with 4 days off. This system employs a cycle system distantly akin to that of the 8-Day Week: two cycle groups each work 3 days, yielding a 6-day week from an employer's point of view in terms of the use of his assets. Computer operators have been successfully cycled in this manner, working night as well as day shifts, in order to provide continuous use of extremely expensive computer assets for 6 days out of a weekly 7. There have also been experiments with this system in other types of employment.

A third alternative calls for seven 10-hour days of work followed by seven days of leisure. This approach, which has been adopted by a few hospitals, represents an extremely "pure" attempt to allocate usable amounts of leisure time by providing the opportunity for 26 miniature vacations per year.

The final alternative involves the use of staggered hours over the course of a 5-day workweek and 8-hour days. The objectives of staggered hours might be described as being:

1. A reduction in traffic congestion resulting from "spreading out" starting and quitting times for workers from the customary 8 to 4 or 9 to 5, and
2. An attempt to attract and hold labor by making working conditions more palatable in terms of offering them greater freedom and discretion in the performance of their work.

Although all of these alternative systems offer certain improvements over our current arrangement of work and leisure hours, none of them represents a solution to fundamental problems attaching to urban life which have been catalogued here and elsewhere, nor an alternative which can be adopted by the majority of employers. In other words, none of them will happen in time to affect us. This will become evident as each is discussed. This same discussion will yield support, in one form or another, for the concept of the 8-Day Week.

The 4-day 40-hour week has made amazing progress over a short period of time. Much of the credit for its popularity is due to the glaring need for reform on the one hand, and the presence of a champion, working on behalf of this system, on the other. In her book, *4 Days, 40 Hours,* Riva Poor reviews in some detail the results obtained with this approach, and variations of it, by the companies and employees which had dared to experiment with it in its earliest days. Some important results are summarized below:

The firms surveyed and reported upon indicated that their employees worked only 18 minutes less per week than the comparable national average for full-time employees. This fact is noteworthy inasmuch as it indicates a willingness of workers *to actually work longer hours* if doing so can lead to an improvement in the quality of their lives. The fact that these people were willing to undergo a form of hardship—longer hours during workdays in order to achieve a *nonmonetary* reward—is another, but equally valid and significant, way of looking at this finding. There can be no doubt that, at least for the people concerned in this small group of companies, the relative importance of money had declined as the value of other, less tangible elements increased.

Wages themselves tended to remain on a par with those paid to these same employees when they worked a 5-day week. In the large majority of firms covered in Poor's survey, wages remained identical before and after the change. Only one of the twenty-seven companies making a permanent change to a 4/3 week found itself paying lower wages, due to maintenance of hourly pay rates and a slightly shorter average week. A few other firms actually increased wages when they in fact saw a slight increase in hours worked after they adopted this type of revised workweek.

The question of overtime was handled differently from company to company. Another form of overtime—moonlighting—increased substantially when compared to national averages. Although this fact tends to vitiate earlier points made on the subject of nonmonetary rewards, it does not invalidate them since the overwhelming majority of workers involved in this survey *did not moonlight*.

Certain of the companies covered in this survey set up objectives to be accomplished by a switch from a 5/2 to a 4/3 week, for example, reduced absenteeism and improved morale among their employees. The heavy majority of companies reported that these objectives had been realized subsequent to transition from one system to the other.

A few of the companies making the change were unionized. Those that were reported both employee and management satisfaction with the manner in which the transition was carried out and its aftermath. From this evidence, one may glean the notion that organized labor is not irredeemably entrenched in its anti-4-day-week attitude, and that it might even be actively receptive to the

8-Day Week, which offers labor a break in the form of a reduction in weekly working hours.

A very small group of workers—142—who were involved in the change to a 4/3 week reported on in *4 Days, 40 Hours* were quizzed as to whether they experienced transitional difficulties and, if so, what these difficulties were. Among these respondents, only one person out of four indicated having encountered any difficulty whatever in making the adjustment. Among those having problems, women outnumbered men two to one. This discrepancy is not too surprising in light of the fact that many of these women were married (virtually two-thirds of working women are) to men who worked shorter hours 5 days per week elsewhere. The abnormal situation in which these women found themselves, therefore, could be said to underlie their difficulties. This situation would not obtain if the working norm had conformed to their own days and hours.

Encouragingly, those adjustment problems encountered were, for the most part, ironed out with the passage of time.

Of major importance is the fact that less than 15 percent of respondents cited fatigue as a problem. Nonetheless, those who were fatigued by the longer work hours *were unanimously in favor of the new work schedule*. This finding bodes very well for the 8-Day Week, which offers *one more day of rest* between each 4-day 40-hour working stint.

Although discussed earlier, it's worth repeating here that the extra weekend day resulting from a change to a 4/3 week appears to have been put to a variety of constructive, instructive, or harmless uses.

An article in the *Los Angeles Times* cited findings obtained with an American Management Association national survey of 1,056 companies on the subject of the 4/3 week and their relationship to it. The findings of this study were interesting in several respects. At the time of this report—April 1972—143 (14 percent) of the companies were on a 4-day week, 237 were "planning or evaluating" this system, 13 had tried and rejected it, and 663, accounting for 63 percent of all companies surveyed, were not considering it.

The following data were given by the 143 companies following the 4-day schedule at the time of the survey:

	Improved	Deteriorated	Unchanged
Costs	38%	11%	51%
Production	62	3	35
Productivity	66	3	31
Profits	51	4	45
Personnel Administration	20	16	64
Production Scheduling	25	26	49
Vendor Relations	5	1	94
Customer Relations	18	3	79
Public Relations	59	16	*
Employee Relations	69	none	31

* 25 percent were uncertain whether public relations improved or not.

In contrast to the preceding overview, perhaps it would be worthwhile to quote from one company's experience with the 4-day week. Beginning in May 1970, the Equitable Life Assurance Society initiated an experiment at its Staten Island data processing center. Dr. Thomas Vris, Manager, Personnel Research, summarized the results of this experiment in a paper given at a University of Pittsburgh seminar on the 4-day week. Part of his summary follows:

The quality of individual operator performance improved substantially. We were careful to measure the performance of experienced operators on work samples that showed a high degree of stability over time. The average error rate of these job samples dropped 20.6% over the 2-month period. However, the average number of records keyed per hour by these employees did not change significantly.

Attitudes toward work hours improved significantly. Only 53% of the employees expressed favorable attitudes toward work hours on a survey conducted before the introduction of the 4-day week. . . . In the follow-up survey at the end of the experimental period, 86% were favorable toward the new pattern of work hours.

Heartened by this experience, Equitable went on to an experiment involving white-collar workers. This experiment proved to be generally satisfactory in terms of work output, attitudes, and absenteeism. *An unexpected by-product appeared in the form of faster development of lower management.*

The foregoing examples and surveys tend to be encouraging as indicators of fairly widespread management willingness to make an effort to improve their employees' lot while, in limited applications, making corporate ends meet. Unfortunately, the 4-day week does not represent an answer for the overwhelming majority of employers or their employees.

Pointing out the shortcomings inherent in a system which is exciting, which is popular, and which is specifically designed to make our lives more livable is not a pleasant task. Nor is it likely to be greeted with enthusiasm by those individuals who have sincerely and urgently advocated such a system, or by those companies which have "laid it on the line" by adopting it. Nonetheless, here are the reasons why a 4/3 week will not become the norm.

1. *Less for more*—Widespread adoption of the 4-day week would tend to encourage the "Less for More" syndrome which already grips us. Rather than acting to even out the load placed on public and quasi-public facilities such as transportation, power, and communications, the 4-day week would tend to perpetuate and increase the strain placed upon them. Traffic jams would move from Friday to Thursday, and worsen in the process, as more people attempted to leave town for longer weekends. Such pressure would, in turn, tend to lead to another tremendous round of road-building, accompanied by the civic need to generate funds through increased taxation.

   In the private sector, tremendous new capital investment would need to be made in an attempt to outrace the cost of producing goods and services at competitive prices. Aside from requiring technological breakthroughs in many productive sectors, such massive replacement of productive capital would be unnecessarily wasteful, coming as it would at a time when this country and the world would be better advised to husband its resources.

2. *In short*—The 4-day week does not bode well as a viable alternative to our present system due to its failure to come to grips with fundamental problems besetting an urbanized society having a capital-intensive economy. Rather, it doggedly, if admirably, limits itself to pursuit of a social ideal without giving adequate consideration to basic socioeconomic elements such as those touched on above. Such problems and shortcomings as these probably underlie one expert's estimate that by 1990, only 35 to 40 percent of the work force will be converted to the 4-day week. By 1990, most of today's working adults will be retired or dead, so you and I will miss the chance to benefit from this system's promise of increased leisure.

3. *On the other hand*—Experiments with the 4-day week have generated tremendous amounts of interest in and study of alternative ways of improving our lives while getting the work done. It has caused a vast amount of intellectual effort to be focused on the interrelated problems of urban crowding, working conditions, employee rewards, and productivity. It has paved the way for masses of concerned individuals to seek and recognize a viable alternative to today's situation. In this respect, the 4-day week has been a tremendous success.

The second alternative system which merits discussion is the 3-day workweek employing 12-hour shifts. The Equitable Life Assurance Society adopted this approach successfully for certain computer operations, as the following excerpt from Vris's analysis indicates:

The 3-day shift is still going strong after almost 5 years of continuous operation . . . the fact that the machine utilization objective was met, and that there was no difficulty in staffing the operation with capable people, is indicative of its success. . . .

The 3-day shift involves about 300 employees. This number represents only a small fraction of the total number of Equitable employees. And the nature of the work, which is machine-based, can hardly be considered typical.

Another company, Thomas J. Lipton, appears to have had far less satisfactory experience in a manufacturing situation where both men and women worked a rotating series of night and day shifts. The following excerpts from a *New York Times* article, published roughly three weeks after these new hours were adopted, fairly represent the problems that had been encountered during the earliest stages:

> Interviews with more than a score of workers in Flemington indicated strong opposition to the new schedule.
> They cited what they considered the debilitating effects of 12 hours of work. . . .
> Those generally opposed were fathers of preschool children and married women who objected to 12-hour swing shifts during which they failed to see their husbands or their school-age children.

Unless they were absolutely necessary, 12-hour days would seem to carry strong disadvantages which tend to offset their benefits. Fatigue and social dislocation appear to be substantial—although the latter might not prove as much a problem if everyone were involved in such a work pattern. It would also carry another potential drawback with it into broad-scale applications—those scheduled to work Saturdays could be expected to strive for different scheduling in order to free their weekends for leisure. Such competition for weekends could lead to a fractious situation between employees and employers and among the employees themselves, or to absenteeism on Saturdays.

Such difficulties as these may constitute the reason why, to date, interest in the 3-day week has been very limited.

The 7-day week, followed by a leisure week, strikes one as an even more extreme and improbable alternative. Although this approach carries with it intriguing possibilities of extended travel, or frequent excursions during the leisure periods, and passes functional tests in hospitals, it doesn't appear promising in the context of general business applications. Most especially, the concept of two shifts alternating over 7-day periods fails the "communications" test. People would not be able to meet and discuss business as they have become accustomed to do. All communications would be "remote" among those who were on opposed cycles. Seven-on, 7-off shifting would probably lead to chaos.

Staggered hours, the last-mentioned alternative, will also fail to solve our problems. At best, it is a half-measure inadequate to solving a set of basic problems requiring more fundamental change to reach a solution. In addition, it seems improbable that part of the working population would willingly accept less-desirable hours, e.g., 7:30 to 3:30 or 10:30 to 6:30, than their otherwise coequal fellow workers. The suggestion of staggered hours strikes me as being more typical of a political gesture than a reasoned and sincere effort to improve the quality of our lives.

10 8-Day Economics

■

*Possible Effects on Productivity in Government and
Private Industry; International Competitiveness;
Unemployment; The Cost of Social Overhead; Pollution*

Although earlier chapters touched occasionally on economic questions, they concentrated, for the most part, on the shortcomings of our current system, or the benefits of the 8-Day Week, *in terms of meeting human needs.* Great as such benefits may have been shown to be, they will fail to become realities, hence amount to absolutely nothing, unless there are indications of The Alternative's viability as part of an economic system. This book is cast in the context of the United States. Thus, economic discussion will relate to its current situation, its system, and its peculiarities. The values which may accrue to it, however, due to adoption of the 8-Day Week would also apply, in a general way, to other countries whose economies are *capital intensive,* that is, heavily reliant on efficient, but costly, productive facilities as opposed to raw labor. Some other countries would be Great Britain, Sweden, Germany, and even Soviet Russia, among others.

For the time being, the United States' economy appears to be stymied by a continuing problem in the area of productivity. Manufacturers either cannot afford to purchase factory equipment that is sufficiently efficient to offset rising labor costs, or such equipment does not exist. Service industries are failing to devise means of improving their employees' output at a rate equal to the cost of employing them. As a partial result of this inability to keep pace, we have inflation, we have a "hardening" unemployment problem, and we are encountering increasing difficulty in competing for world trade. *Business Week* summarized the problem of un-realized improvements in productivity along the following lines in an issue devoted to that subject:

> Five years of inflation, recession, and uncertain recovery have forced the men who manage U.S. business and the men who make U.S. economic policy to a painful conclusion: How the nation must make a quantum jump in efficiency. It must get more output from its men and machines. It must offset rising wage costs with higher production per worker. It must expand its income not just by increasing the inputs of labor and capital but also by increasing the effectiveness of these inputs. . . .
>
> Devaluation of the dollar, Phase II wage-price controls, and the 1972 upturn of the economy provided some temporary relief. They have not produced any long-term answers. The U.S. still must find a way to achieve continuing growth without inflation, to meet the challenge of foreign competitors, and to provide for the ever-growing needs of a complex, urbanized society without overcommitting its economic resources. . . .
>
> . . . when everything else is done, the fact remains that if the U.S. is to get what it wants, it must get more production out of each unit of capital and labor it puts through its economic system.

Generally speaking, when people think or talk about productivity, they tend to emphasize the labor aspect, as in, "How can I get more out of my workers?" Such a reflex attitude tends to ignore the fact that other elements besides people are involved in the production of goods or performance of services. Overemphasis on the effect of *labor* productivity tends to distort the true question of productivity, which might be better stated as, "How can I get more out of my capital (in the form of land, building, machines, and money) and labor?" Since it is very difficult to devise a formula which assigns the correct value to each of these items in combination, the simpler concept of partial productivity, e.g., labor, is used. In a country having tremendous capital and productive resources at its disposal, such a practice can lead to deceptive results.

One economist who realizes this is Professor John Kendrick of George Washington University. In estimating the contribution to economic growth by various factors, he concluded that a considerable portion of economic growth resulting from "labor productivity" was really due to increased inputs of capital per man-hour. Such a conclusion would seem to make sense when one considers the fact that the reason an employer buys a machine in the first place is to help his employees accomplish more in a given work day.

The lack of growth in productivity, in the sense of using what is available to greatest advantage, is probably the greatest single source underlying our economy's failure to show vitality over the period 1967–72.

One significant offshoot of this relative weakness in productivity growth is unemployment. At the same time, unemployment contributes to losses in real economic growth. Edward Denison of the Brookings Institution has attempted to identify the causes of growth in a country's economy and to determine the exact amount of this growth attributable to each of these causes. In a study of U.S. economic growth between 1950 and 1962, he identified employment growth as the single most important contributor to over-all economic progress, accounting for over one-fourth of the total. A consumer who is prepared to assume that role because he is employed can clearly have an effect on the growth of the economy in which he plays a part. A consumer who is *not* prepared to play such a role because he is unemployed or underemployed cannot be expected to make such a positive contribution because of his failure to produce valuable goods or services and his inability to relate fully to others' work due to his own limited purchasing power.

In this country, the core of unemployment seems to be hardening in the range of 5 to 5½ percent. This level is considered to be fairly high by responsible and authoritative economists and other interested members of society, such as politicians. Possibly more interested than either of these groups, however, are the unemployed themselves, who are finding great difficulty in replacing lost employment. Between 1969 and 1971, total unemployment levels increased approximately 68 percent. At the same time, the percentage of unemployed blue-collar workers unable to find work within fifteen weeks of prior job loss increased 106 percent; white-collar workers having the same problem increased 85 percent; members of the professional and managerial class unable to find work within fifteen weeks of job loss increased 88 percent. Such semipermanent job dispossession can be expected not only to dismay several million would-be breadwinners but also to cost money in the form of: (1) unrealized contributions to the economy and (2) public support funds.

Although improved education levels are believed by Mr. Denison to make a significant contribution to a country's economic growth, it is clear that, these days, a degree is no guarantee of employment for the holder. A survey of several hundred major employers conducted by the College Placement Council indicated that these companies hired approximately 70,000 college graduates in 1970, but only 50,000 in 1972, when more seniors were graduated. The American Bar Association has estimated that in 1972, the number of law school graduates exceeded the number of jobs available to them by 10,000. It has been estimated that by 1980, one out of five graduates will be forced to take jobs beneath their training— that 1.5 to 2.5 million people will not be able to apply what they have learned, despite their expectations to the contrary. If such estimates as these are accurate, the country faces an unhappy economic outlook, accompanied by the potential for considerable political turmoil, for many years to come.

A third economic fact which appears relevant to the 8-Day Week is that of persistent inflation. During the boom years of the early

1960s, a number of technical breakthroughs were achieved, allowing industry to enjoy a relative outburst in worker productivity and employees themselves to achieve large pay raises. While the era of increased productivity was fairly short-lived, the attitude toward pay increases that it spawned persisted beyond the point where such demands continued to be "justified" by renewed gains in productivity. The only way in which employers could accommodate such latter-day demands, while maintaining or increasing dollar profit levels, was through increasing prices for the goods and services their firms provided. By raising prices, industry tended to devalue the wage increases won by their employees, with the result that another wage-price increase cycle was encouraged, and inflation abetted, to the point where runaway inflation emerged as a distinct possibility. Phase I and Phase II wage-price restrictions were invoked to avert such a catastrophe by attempting to limit the extent to which wages and prices could be increased. Well-intended and somewhat effective as these restraints may have been, they constituted no permanent solution to the problem of real or potential inflation. Unless a way can be found to put capital to more productive use, the threat of substantial inflation will join with that of continued high levels of unemployment to menace economic stability worldwide.

Inflation's impact on this country's ability to compete in world markets has been substantial. The year 1971 was the first in approximately eighty years in which the U.S. had a negative balance of trade, that is, it imported considerably more than it exported. A basic reason for this trade imbalance was the inability to compete with foreign producers in terms of delivering value for money equal to their own offerings. Such inability to compete effectively at home and abroad was not limited merely to cameras, transistor radios, autos, and television sets, but also began to include products formerly considered to be under the more or less exclusive control of U.S. companies, which hitherto had enjoyed a technological lead over foreign competitors. The following excerpts from the *Wall*

Street Journal indicate in a limited way how the nature of foreign competition can change:

> During the 1970's, America can expect coming out of the Japanese islands products that depend more on technology than price, more on high value than mass production, more on domestic brainpower than on imported raw materials.
>
> . . . Nippon Electric Corp., for instance, is a major factor in international communications, selling more satellite ground stations than all other companies in the world.
>
> . . . There will be a big market for equipment for offshore mining. Komatsu has built a model of a bulldozer that works 200 feet below water, and it thinks it is alone in this field.
>
> . . . A few weeks ago several Japanese concerns signed a $171 million contract with Argentina for a complete overhaul of that country's railroad system. . . .
>
> . . . "Five years ago Japanese construction equipment wasn't very strong abroad," recalls Kanichi Uchida, technical director. "We had a reputation for poor quality and breakdowns. Now we have 30% of the world market."

As productivity lagged, inflation surged, unemployment persisted, and our ability to compete abroad lessened, the cost of social overhead—public costs of all sorts—rose astoundingly. Between 1960 and 1970, per capita taxes nearly doubled to nearly $1,400 per year for every man, woman, and child. Despite such a tremendous revenue, governments at all levels found themselves unable to meet financial demands from current revenues. As a result, they have borrowed heavily—$60 billion in 1970 alone, for instance. Such borrowing creates another tremendous cost item in government budgets, in the form of debt repayment and interest expense. Such debt service is now the third largest public expense item after defense and education. It has been estimated by a New York University finance professor, Lawrence S. Ritter, that between 1972 and 1980, public spending will be *$46 billion per year more* than the 1970 level to meet only four of many social needs: (1) improved mass transit; (2) pollution control; (3) law enforcement; (4) education. Over nine years' time, that comes to a *$414 billion increase*. Obviously, revenues will fail to keep pace with such increases in spending, with the result that if the money is to be spent, the governments spending it will be forced to borrow further by floating bond issues.

The average citizen, already taxed to distraction, does not appear to be sympathetic to such increases in spending, moving when possible to prevent passage of further bond issues by voting them down. In 1971, citizens voted down 65 percent of all proposed bond issues. Voting "No" is the citizen's inarticulate way of passing the civic buck back to administrators (rather than handing it over to them) in the form of a demand for greater productivity per dollar spent on government and government-managed activities. The voter's reach, however, is limited essentially to the state and local spending levels. The federal budget accrued an $87 billion increased deficit between fiscal years 1971 and 1973, at least part of which resulted from tremendous inflation in government construction, the Vietnam war, below-plan tax revenues stemming from recession, and the cost of aiding unexpected numbers of unemployed.

City and state governments are equally penurious. New York State appears to be over $8 billion in debt, and paying $600 million per year to service that debt. New York City can't make ends meet on a $10 billion budget; Detroit is deeply in the red and the rest of the country's states and municipalities are encountering financial difficulties.

The problems of social overhead which our country and we, the taxpayers, face—along with such other problems as inflation, unemployment, and lack of growth in productivity—all appear to be soluble through adoption of the 8-Day Week.

Basically, this solution lies in making greater use of already available assets on the one hand, and tending to fill the void of unemployment on the other. This process will tend to stanch the financial hemorrhage flowing from government coffers into massive, and apparently unending, new construction projects, will encourage private industry to concentrate on its most productive assets, and will make better use of available brainpower—an effective contributor to real economic growth and stability.

Because government is such big business, employing approximately 19 percent of the entire work force, perhaps it merits first place in discussing the 8-Day Week's potential economic impact.

The first influence The Alternative could have on the productivity of government operations would be in the relatively mundane area of providing work space for government employees. If even one-third of the country's 16 million civil servants could be induced to share office space, parking places, typewriters, cafeterias, and so on as a result of working different 4-day cycles, the cost of constructing new office space and attendant facilities could be substantially eliminated. Government-occupied office buildings are at least as expensive as those occupied by members of private industry. I don't know how much money is being or has been spent at all levels of government to house civil employees, but some clue as to the savings available through greater use of existing facilities may be found in the cost of new government office buildings on Pennsylvania Avenue in Washington: (1) the Rayburn Building cost between $87 and $100 million; (2) the new FBI building is being built at an estimated cost of $126 million; (3) the Federal Triangle, across the street from the FBI's new home, came in at $135 million. These add up to more than a third of a billion dollars. It is interesting to note that when the FBI building was originally planned in 1962, its cost was estimated at $60 million. Since then, an additional $38 million, or 67 percent, has been added to cover the cost of inflation between then and 1974, its projected completion date. The remaining difference, another $28 million, is apparently allocable to changes in design.

Housing government employees, however, is merely a starting point. Other areas in which various governments carry heavy spending power appear to offer even greater, nonrecessionary savings potential.

One potentially rich source of increased productivity through better use, and reduced spending, can be found in transportation, i.e., highways and mass transit systems. The interstate highway system will have cost $76 billion when completed. Roadways cover approximately 21 million acres of land. It costs approximately $5 million per mile to construct new interstate roads. It would seem that by halving the peak workday pressure on urban highway systems, city streets, tunnels, and bridges, these same facilities would immediately prove more nearly, if not entirely, adequate to handle the traffic burden imposed upon them. It seems logical to assume that if half the work force is allowed to stay home on any given day, they will tend to avoid rush-hour traffic by virtue of having no reason to take part in it.

A second area in which government-originated spending might be reduced substantially is that of mass transit systems, a number of which are being studied, planned, or built during the 1970s. Although mass transit systems such as subways or other high-speed rail facilities are popularly perceived as being "good" in the sense of their being less polluting than automobiles, plus their ability to bypass tremendous masses of traffic due to their exclusive routing, their value would definitely bear restudy in light of the altered traffic circumstances that would be brought about by the 8-Day Week. If traffic congestion is the main reason for such systems' being, then removal of congestion should logically vitiate or entirely eliminate the need for them.

A significant reduction in spending on transportation facilities of various kinds could lead to reallocation of significant sums of government funds to other uses, including: (1) medicine and medical facilities; (2) education (teachers' salaries); (3) reduction of debt and debt service; (4) stabilized or reduced taxes.

Another example of how government could relate to and the people benefit from the 8-Day Week may be found in education. Through use of classroom and campus facilities on a virtually year-round basis, a great reduction in school construction could apparently take place, with spending emphasis shifting to payment of a substantially increased teaching staff. *Business Week* states that the total budgets for higher education increased sixfold between 1956 and 1972, from $4.6 billion to $28 billion per year. It also states that "most colleges are cutting down on faculty, not adding to it." It is obvious that this sixfold increase did not all go into salary increases for professors; much of it had to have gone into campus construction and maintenance. Bearing in mind that we have, and will have, an overabundance of people qualified for teaching, it would seem reasonable to conclude that continuous use of school facilities would: (1) substantially reduce construction costs and attendant debt service; (2) allow a virtual doubling in the number of teachers; (3) reduce unemployment, hence (4) reduce unemployment-related government spending while increasing government income by expanding or improving the quality of the tax base; (5) stabilize or reduce taxes. Each $1 billion reallocated from construction to salaries could mean 100,000 jobs for teachers at an annual salary of $10,000.

A further effect which might be felt by governments and taxpayers could conceivably take place in crime, crime prevention, and public safety. The absence of uniform, essentially universal business hours such as we have now would make it difficult for potential daylight burglars to be assured that a home or apartment would be empty on any given day. The lack of such certainty should encourage more circumspection on the criminal's part, hence possibly reduce the number of unplanned or "ad hoc" crimes.

On the other hand, those criminals specializing in industrial theft, who steal office and factory equipment and machinery, would have no days and fewer nighttime hours in which to work unmolested by employees. Keeping an office open 70 hours per week, rather than the current 40, would tend to reduce the opportunity for sneak thieves to enter unchallenged by responsible employees. If this effect were to come about, the level of certain police activity—that is, guarding against and seeking burglars—might also decline.

In a similar vein, certain types of police activity related to the handling of heavy traffic should also be eased by reduced vehicular and population pressure within urban areas on an average day. Reduced traffic congestion per se would also increase police mobility in their efforts to answer calls.

Depending on how these elements were related to in combination, several outcomes could occur: (1) the cost of certain types of crime could be reduced; (2) crime rates themselves might be reduced; (3) the cost of police work might be stabilized; (4) taxes allocated to the control of crime might either stabilize or be reduced.

A related subject—jails and due process—could also be affected. As with schools, continuous use of courtroom facilities could be made by doubling the number of judges sitting in civil and criminal courts. An increase in the number of judges sitting could: (1) reduce the tremendous docket backlog faced by all levels of jurisprudence from coast to coast; (2) reduce the time spent in jail awaiting trial by urban prisoners unable to post bail and lessen the state cost of supporting them; (3) reduce the level of jail crowding, which is commonly believed to have a deleterious effect on humans *qua* future members of society; (4) reduce the need for new jail construction; (5) reduce unemployment among those people having training in the law; (6) stabilize or reduce taxes allocated to "the administration of justice." It may be worth pointing out here that New York City's 1972–73 budget allocates nearly $1 billion to "the administration of justice."

The basic thrust of all the foregoing tends to be toward the greater use of available government-owned or -controlled assets, reduced emphasis on construction of new assets, and a redirection of emphasis toward performance of services, while attacking the problem of unemployment.

The effects of the 8-Day Week on the private sector of the economy are at least equally interesting. The key to success or failure in terms of achieving either real economic growth or stability without inordinate unemployment may be said to lie in how capital is viewed and whether it is used to maximize productivity while minimizing waste in various forms. The following excerpt from *Business Week* is highly suitable as background for subsequent discussion of The Alternative's effects on manufacturing and certain types of capital-intensive services:

> Yet the hard fact is that 15% of manufacturing facilities operated by large U.S. companies were technologically obsolete at the end of 1970, and a substantial portion of the other 85% was not competitive in the face of rising labor costs.

Implicit in this statement is the fact that across the spectrum of manufacturing companies, there exist certain productive assets which are *relatively efficient* and certain others which are *relatively inefficient*. The existence of this relatively efficient and inefficient capacity probably does not break down along company lines—that is, Company A does not possess only modern, highly productive facilities, and Company B does not possess equipment which is exclusively obsolete. Rather, each firm is likely to possess a little of both types, with the majority of its capacity being neither ultra-productive nor unproductive. The tremendous number of mergers, and the formation of conglomerate companies, will have tended to make this supposition increasingly true with the passage of time.

Given this situation, a manufacturer could, if circumstances permitted, concentrate activities upon that portion of his capacity (or those companies in his conglomerate) which was relatively more efficient, and accelerate the elimination or replacement of his less efficient capacity. This could be accomplished by increasing the man-hours applied to use of his more efficient—i.e., profitable—capacity, which would tend to underwrite the cost of rapidly depreciating or scrapping unproductive capacity. Workers formerly engaged in unproductive operations could be redeployed to man the company's more productive assets, in the form of the new second cycle group.

Such an approach is implicit in the experience of two companies, one taken from an accounting point of view, the other on the basis of production—both reported upon in *Business Week.*

William W. Bewley, Jr., corporate economist of Hercules, Inc., analyzed the performance of his company's major profit centers in terms of revenues they generated compared to the costs they represented, broken down among labor, fixed capital, and working capital. He determined that 70 to 80 percent of the company's over-all productivity gains stemmed from capital investment and technological improvements. He also found that 90 percent of all productivity gains over ten years had come from three product areas. Since this company manufactures some 1,200 products, it can be deduced from the above that in many of its manufacturing activities, the company was marching in place, at best, if not actually losing ground. Had these discoveries been made sooner, the company would have been able to concentrate its capital against profitable activities and reconsider its other, unproductive pursuits.

In a plant situation, Black & Decker Mfg. Co. concentrates its effort against continually improving its mechanized processes to increase its productivity, while retaining rather than dispossessing its employees. The company can accomplish such a feat because, with each improvement in efficiency, it is able to offer consumers greater value for money, thus increasing sales, while earning a profit for itself. If Black & Decker had raised prices in line with inflation, the drill it offered at $16.95 in 1946 would now cost approximately $30, rather than the actual current retail price of $7.99.

The philosophy of using capital more fully (as in the case of Black & Decker) or more "intelligently" (as in the case of Hercules) dovetails with the concept of the 8-Day Week. Institution of this system would encourage greater use of more productive assets without the need for paying overtime wages. Capital now employed 40 hours per week could be put to productive use 70 hours under the 8-Day Week—a 75 percent increase. Although it might at first appear that a tremendous overcapacity situation would result, this is seen not to be the case when one remembers that marginal plants will be closed in favor of those which are more productive, and labor forces shifted accordingly. The over-all effect of such shifting in manufacturing emphasis is twofold:

1. There would be a tendency to upgrade productivity by making greater use of newer equipment—a move which would have the same effect as investment in new capital but which would not carry with it the cost of investing in additional new capacity;
2. The acquisition of new capacity to meet demand could be postponed because of the greater use of current productive resources.

Certain companies require economies of scale in order to produce their products at competitive prices. When demand begins to exceed their capacity, they are therefore forced to make massive investments in new capacity which will lie idle until demand catches up. The ability to "stretch" capacity, outlined above, should appeal to such companies.

Widespread shifting of manpower toward more productive assets by industry could be expected to lead to stabilized costs—and prices—for output, thus tending to slow or arrest inflation. In the process, the need for employees to demand and get large wage increases to offset losses in purchasing power due to inflation would tend to be diminished, while raises which they might obtain over time would represent true increases in real income. At the same time, such price stability domestically could lead fairly quickly to a reversal of the current trend toward imports' exceeding exports. As prices for manufactured goods stabilized, demand would presumably swing toward domestic products as their price-value relationships improved. In a similar vein, U.S.-produced goods would tend to become more competitive in export markets, thus further encouraging a balancing effect on total international commerce.

Certain service industries employ a great deal of capital in the process of providing such service. The airline industry constitutes an excellent example. U.S. airlines invested a tremendous amount of money in new equipment between 1960 and 1970, treading a razor's edge between the efficiency of operating large jet aircraft and their enormous cost. During that decade, gross investment rose 254 percent; available seat miles increased 304 percent; revenue passenger miles gained 238 percent, and while the load factor slipped by approximately one-sixth, from 59.3 percent to 49.7 percent, the number of *empty seat-miles increased 402 percent*. The cost of the increase in empty seat-milès has to be reflected in the price of an airline ticket. Given that fact, it would not seem a very daring speculation to presume that airline load factors, total revenues, and profits would react significantly to a situation in which people's usable leisure days were increased sharply. It could be that load factors would increase sufficiently to allow for substantial reductions in ticket prices, leading, in turn, to a modest revolution in air travel.

Other highly capitalized service industries, such as trucking, might also conceivably benefit from greater utilization of capital as well as increased operating efficiencies due to the greater speed with which trucks could pass into and out of cities as they picked up or delivered goods. A similar effect would probably also be felt by lessees of all types, including businesses leasing heavy equipment, fleet vehicles, and office space.

Telephone companies, such as AT&T, have made tremendous investments in equipment and appear to suffer from an insatiable need for new capital through the 1970s and beyond. A minor example of the 8-Day Week's effect can be made of New York Telephone's operations in New York City and how these operations might be altered. On the average business day, 15 million telephone calls were found to be made in Manhattan alone. This level drops to 5.4 million calls on average Saturdays and 4.3 million on Sundays. In order to accommodate current peak usage rates, New York Telephone should probably be equipped to handle somewhat more than the average number of business day calls—perhaps 20 million calls. Thus, the company finds itself in the position of having to provide peak capacity roughly five times as great as the levels of Sunday's "trough" rate of use. Subscribers, at the same time, encounter frequent difficulties placing a call during workdays because of overloaded circuits. This situation might resolve itself through division of the work force and reduction of the average "business day" load by spreading that load over 7 days, rather than 5. If the total number of weekly calls (85 million) were redistributed evenly, average daily usage would amount to approximately 12 million calls—a level which AT&T is equipped to handle. The supposition here is that in New York and other major urban areas, AT&T's service would improve from a functional point of view; efficiency of the company's operations would increase; requirements for new capital would decrease; the cost of service would tend to be stabilized if not actually reduced as federally regulated company profits increased.

Certain types of companies, such as advertising agencies or insurance companies, have a substantial portion of their expenses allocable to rent and salaries. By adopting the 8-Day Week, such companies would, along with others, be effectively raising hourly pay rates in proportion to the reduction in the number of hours worked per week by their employees. If such companies are currently on a 40-hour week, this per-hour raise would amount to 12½ percent. On the surface, such an increase in *pay rates,* as opposed to *total wages, which would remain the same,* might appear to be unaffordable. Such is probably not the case, however. If leased space is viewed as an asset, the concept of maximizing the use of assets can be employed to reduce operating costs, hence increase employee productivity. Since only half as many employees would be present at work on any given day, their employers would not be required to lease as much space as was formerly necessary. Depending on the type of company involved and the nature of that company's work force, space needs could be reduced to a theoretical limit of 50 percent. A similar effect would take place in terms of office equipment needs, such as telephones, calculators, typewriters, and derivative costs for such equipment, including insurance and service contracts.

All of the foregoing is meant to outline how a variety of economic factors and different types of businesses might be affected by adoption of the 8-Day Week. At the same time as such benefits, reactions, and adjustments took place, a number of present-day situations would probably be altered, certain shifts would take place, and some side effects would be felt.

There would probably be a decided shift in real estate values, from urban to rural, due to a lessening in pressure for office space and the increase in time available for people to enjoy country life. At the same time, urban construction would presumably decline, while individual-unit rural construction showed a dramatic increase.

A wide variety of leisure-oriented industries, including airlines, resort areas, manufacturers of sporting goods, entertainment industries, and publishers would encounter strong growth in demand. In fact, the growth in leisure-related industries could be unlike anything in their past experience.

Demand for certain basic industries' products, like steel and automobiles, would probably increase.

Certain other basic industries, such as machine-tool manufacturing, would probably encounter a temporary lessening in demand as their industrial customers made greater use of already available productive capacity. This situation, on the other hand, should reverse itself, over time, as technological breakthroughs led to "new generations" in machine-based productivity.

The trend toward pollution control might be hastened by adoption of the 8-Day Week. It has been estimated by Chase

Econometrics Associates, a Chase Manhattan Bank subsidiary, that between 200 and 300 plants will be closed by 1976 due to their failure to meet antipollution standards. In this study, most of these plants were described as being already marginal from a productivity point of view. In essence, then, pollution standards hastened the demise of *relatively unproductive, or inefficient,* facilities. The relationship noted between productive inefficiency and the tendency to pollute should carry over to other plants, which would be closed voluntarily by companies as the 8-Day Week made possible the greater use of facilities that were both more productive and less pollutive.

At the same time, urban vehicular pollution might be expected to be reduced. Lighter traffic would allow for lessened point-to-point travel time, along with engine-idling traffic jams. The reduction in vehicular emissions could be expected to be roughly proportionate to the reduction in an individual's average travel time spent going to and from work, performing a round of errands or doing anything else involving car, bus, or truck travel. Since road vehicles are the greatest single source of air pollution, the effect of reduced travel time could prove significant.

The balance-of-trade situation would probably be altered as productivity increased and the prices of exportable goods stabilized. Although several industrialized foreign countries have enjoyed far greater gains in productivity than the U.S. over many years, these countries, also, are encountering rising costs. Their advantage, therefore, could be presumed to be temporary if the U.S. economy were reordered along less inflationary lines while other countries continued their upward trends in production costs. On the other hand, a more productive domestic economy would constitute grounds, in the form of strengthened real purchasing power in the hands of U.S. consumers, for the importation of competitive goods.

The persistent problems of total unemployment levels, accompanied by "hardening" unemployment and job dislocation of large and growing numbers of better-educated job seekers, would tend to be greatly eased or resolved. References have already been made to how more teachers and more lawyers (as judges) would find employment as a result of the 8-Day Week's adoption. To these could be added other "structural" employment directly resulting from the nature of the system. For example, banks would have to hire another set of guards and the postal system more letter carriers. Certain unique functions would require duplication; e.g., a brokerage house employing one municipal bond trader would need two; more office receptionists would be needed; small companies employing a part-time bookkeeper might require more bookkeeping talent.

In a broader sense, it may be fair to presume that growth in many leisure-related industries would create extensive labor demand. At the same time, generally more efficient and more profitable operations among firms not directly affected by leisure demand could lead to their expansion, with the concomitant need for additional personnel. To this could be added general increases in demand stemming from improved economic health and higher employment levels—leading to a further round of employment. Stabilization of international trade would tend to eliminate job losses resulting from the loss of export markets.

The possibilities inherent in the 8-Day Week are felt to be fairly significant. Between 1972 and 1977, the total number of people between the ages of 20 through 25 will increase by 12 percent, from 21 million to 23.7 million. It would seem desirable to have a relatively buoyant economic situation awaiting them at the point in their lives when they tend to form households and are expected to earn a living.

The general economic effect of this system would appear to be in line with its social effects, to wit, rather than stressing and encouraging quantitative growth, the accent would tend to be on the *qualitative* aspects of economic progress. Such emphasis might lead to the realization of a greater degree of real improvement in income levels, while tending to minimize the rate at which capital and natural resources are consumed in achieving this goal.

11 Making It Happen

■

*Our Increasing Flexibility; One Company's Already
Doing It; Necessary Mechanics; Helping Your
Company Change; Spreading the Word;
Where Else but Here?*

The reader of this book might conclude, as he nears its end, that there must be something impossible about, or wrong with, the concepts it contains. Despite the fact that it contains blueprints for making our lives easier, more pleasant, more productive, and even more meaningful, there must be a flaw somewhere.

Ten years ago, such a doubting attitude might have been not only prevalent, but also valid. The tendency to cling to certain established practices is not as strong as it once was, however. People have become more willing to think for themselves, more willing to act in defense or furtherance of their own interests and needs. They have become smarter and more self-reliant. Evidence of this fact is at every hand, and we need not belabor it here beyond one interesting and relevant note. In discussing the concept and workings of the 8-Day Week with perhaps 200 people, I encountered only three who found fault with it. One, a Dutchman, stated a preference for shorter working days rather than more days off. Another said it "sounded too good to be true," which indicated to me that his enthusiasm was tempered by cynicism born of disbelief in a system's (or the establishment's) ability to act wisely, rather than automatically, in response to changing circumstances. The third objection was based on the belief that although The Alternative was absolutely logical, it "wouldn't work unless everybody did it." I didn't understand that comment and still don't.

The remaining 197 people seemed to think that quick adoption of such a system was not only desirable, but *a distinct possibility as well.* Many of these people took the trouble to tear out and mail relevant material, and even wrote short papers to themselves (and me) on how the 8-Day Week would work within their own companies.

This should lend great encouragement to readers interested in enriching their lives in a variety of ways. Still, if such an approach is so logical, and economically viable, why hasn't it been done already? The answer to that question is, *it has been.*

I discovered, after starting this book, that the Cromwell Corporation of South Bend, Indiana, has employed a version of the 8-Day Week since 1966. This discovery was made in the process of researching alternative approaches to the current workweek. In an appendix to *4 Days, 40 Hours,* a report was made by John L. Schohl, founder of the Cromwell Corporation, on his company's approach to reordering work schedules. The following are excerpts from his statement:

1. *Why did he do it?*—"I needed a work schedule which would use as many of the 8,766 hours in the year as I could make attractive to workers."

2. *What form did his approach take?*—"After considering many possibilities, I settled on one I regarded as optimum: two 10-hour shifts a day for two crews of two 10-hour shifts each. One crew (2 shifts) works 4 days while the other is off—alternating in 8-day cycles—4 days on, 4 days off. Operations go on routinely 20 hours a day, 7 days each calendar week—about 7,000 hours a year."

3. *Some smart capitalist math*—"Hourly direct labor costs are increased, but fixed and indirect costs are spread over so many more hours that they are overabsorbed—with the gain

going right to profit. The return on investment in an activity carrying a burden of 250% or more and working 2 conventional 5-day, 40-hour shifts (a situation commonly considered good) can be doubled by going to my schedule."

4. *Advantages to the employer*—"Advantages include lower investment in relation to output than is usual, increases in the velocities of significant factors like turnover of work-in-process and actual wearing out of equipment for favorable earlier replacement, and much easier recruiting."

AND THE WORKERS?

5. *Time off*—"The men have more than half of the days in the year free—coming to work 65 fewer days a year than in an ordinary job. . . . Used imaginatively and aggressively, these conditions of employment can attract men to work they would shun otherwise, like foundry work."

6. *The 35-hour week, a union goal*—"It has not come about widely, because sufficient increases in productivity have not been realized. Companies simply cannot afford to shrink their time bases as they would have to do within the context of the 7-day calendar week. My 8-day week plan compensates by giving the company a high level of utilization while giving the worker greater free time—meeting conditions of present economic realities."

HAS IT SUCCEEDED OVER TIME?

7. *It has, indeed!*—"The machining business I planned began operations during 1966 . . . the version of my plan described here (many variations are possible) was and still is used in this business. The economics of the plan worked out as I expected, and the schedule has been a source of recruiting strength and worker satisfaction."

Although we may regret not having been employed at one of Mr. Schohl's turret lathes since 1966, we do owe thanks to him for having conducted a successful test of the 8-Day Week over a period of years. His experience makes it seem even more possible for the rest of us to achieve this goal. The remainder of this chapter is devoted to outlining what needs to happen, in a mechanical sense, for the 8-Day Week to function; how major employers can affect its progress toward adoption, and how you, an individual, can help make it come about.

In order to carry on commerce, any company wishing to adopt the 8-Day Week would benefit greatly from having certain commerce-related institutions also open every day of the week. Primary among these institutions appear to be banks and the postal service. To these might perhaps be added the various stock and commodity exchanges, although their relative importance would vary considerably from business to business. All commerce-related major facilities, e.g., telephone service and transportation, already function constantly. Many, if not most, banks and post offices are open Saturdays, if only for a partial day. The adjustment required in their business schedule would not, therefore, be a major one.

Another institution of a different type would also have to be adjusted to enable a company to adopt the 8-Day Week. Laws which either prohibit women from working more than 8 hours a day, or which require overtime payment for hours worked beyond 8, for reasons of sex or other bases (e.g., Walsh-Healey), would have to be repealed or modified so as not to handicap an employer willing to give his workers half the year off. "Blue laws" forbidding various types of business activities from taking place on Sundays would have to go, or employers would be liable to repeated fines for their infraction. In this connection, perhaps it is worth noting that blue laws once served the purpose of protecting labor from management avarice expressed in the form of demands that employees work Sundays as well as all other days of the week. Their usefulness, in this respect, has therefore been outlived as labor progressed to a customary 5-day week and management has become accustomed to relating increasingly to the needs, as well as the power, of employees.

Once the legal and commercial "basics" were established, any company wishing to profit from the 8-Day Week could do so. Desirable leadership in a general movement to The Alternative, however, could be provided by those companies and other employers which are responsible for a tremendous percentage of total employment as well as the greater part of the economy's productive and other assets.

Various governmental agencies alone account for roughly one-fifth of all jobs held in this country. Obviously, the decision to adopt the new system for civil employees would lend tremendous impetus to similar adoption by members of the economy's private sector. Among the latter, those most likely to be susceptible to the values of the 8-Day Week from a productivity point of view are the country's largest companies. The top 200 corporations control approximately 60 percent of private industry's total productive assets. It is these companies that are most troubled by antipollution regulations on the one hand, and a productivity squeeze on the other. By relating to the opportunities inherent in change to the recommended system, they could, to all intents and purposes, make the 8-Day Week a national reality. Although the management of such companies may be said to be well informed and interested in social as well as financial progress, their interest in and progress toward adoption of the 8-Day Week should not simply be assumed and awaited. Such stimulus best comes from individuals who both desire a better life style and are concerned with economic facts.

My advice to such individuals breaks down into several parts. First, go back to page 1 and start again. Short as it may be, this book contains a broad range of facts and topics with which the reader should be relatively familiar if he or she is to put them to effective use. Having a firm grasp on the facts and philosophy is a tremendous aid to an individual who would discuss any subject intelligently and convincingly with his fellows. Since the 8-Day Week may seem to carry a superficial resemblance to the 4-day 40-hour week, it is essential that the reader be able to distinguish between the two, and clearly understand how the 8-Day Week would operate. For this reason, the outline of its workings, given in Chapter 2, is repeated below:

First, let us *revise the workweek* so that businesses and related activities may remain open and going

- TEN HOURS PER DAY
- SEVEN DAYS PER WEEK

Second, let us *divide the work force* so that, on any given day,

- ONE-HALF OF THE PEOPLE ARE WORKING
- ONE-HALF OF THE PEOPLE ARE OFF

Third, let us *restructure the relationship between our periods of work and our leisure time*, so that each person

- WORKS FOR FOUR DAYS
         and
- TAKES THE NEXT FOUR DAYS OFF

Fourth, to avert catastrophic traffic jams and *to maintain a smoothly functioning business mechanism,* let workers' "on" and "off" periods be staggered evenly throughout 8-day cycles so that *each day*

- ONE-EIGHTH OF WORKING PEOPLE RETURN TO WORK
         while
- ONE-EIGHTH OF US BEGIN A REST CYCLE

Having mastered the above, and thoroughly acquainted yourself with its meanings and implications, you are ready to take the next step. This is to be positive and flexible in your thinking. There was a time when things took an awfully long time to happen, simply because established thinking *really was established.* That era is over. We are readier now to learn and be adaptable as a people. We have become able to actually listen to and consider nonestablishment notions.

Such flexibility represents a major key to modern man's ability to survive a variety of pressures and changes which play an increasing part in daily life. Maintenance of this flexibility, however, requires the expenditure of a certain amount of energy—and additional effort is required whenever this flexibility takes the form of breaking new ground.

In other words, if you wish to help make the 8-Day Week a reality, you must be strong, as well as mentally prepared. Although most of us still tend to shun the label, we must become activists in large numbers if desired reform is to take place. Fortunately, activism need not be crude, unpleasant, stupid, or tasteless to be activism. There are ways and places to wage an effective word-of-mouth campaign; for example, while commuting to work; during coffee breaks; at PTA meetings; during lunchtime; at the bowling alley or the 19th hole; during Sunday brunch.

My personal experience on the subject should reassure you that you will encounter very little resistance to the idea of the 8-Day Week. You may encounter doubt, skepticism, vagueness, stupidity, and laziness, but very few people will be capable of finding fault with a system which is neocapitalism at its best; whose fundamental thrust is toward a significant improvement in the quality of our lives. None of that Republican/Democrat, pro- or anti-school tax business to contend with. Only cynicism, inertia, uncertainty, and skepticism. And how does one deal with these elements whose taproots all drink from the pool of personal insecurity? By being confident on the subject.

Everybody knows the value of self-confidence in interpersonal relationships, how the person with an air of competence commands more listening room and deference. Everybody, on the other hand, knows how easy it is to poke holes in an idea. Nobody enjoys the thought of making an ass of himself in front of his peers. Combine these elements and you arrive at the indicated action: reread this book as many times as is necessary to feel comfortable with its suggestions, rationales, and facts.

As you do so, concentrate on the weak points as you see them and work out *your own* way of making them stronger, more supportable, more realistic or intelligent. It will help make your arguments most coherent if you can cover the range from the general to the specific—so read the book and form your approach at different levels of intensity. Consider the subject from the broadest possible view first, *then* get down to your own cases.

It is at this latter point that you should begin to see how the 8-Day Week can be made to apply to *your own* life, *your own* job.

Now you are ready to go out and proselytize.

Perhaps you should practice your preaching first before a relatively sympathetic audience. Husbands, wives, children, and close friends should all prove good listeners. As you practice, you'll probably notice a pattern of questions or hesitations emerge— you'll also notice a tremendous amount of interest and enthusiasm —which you will eventually tend to anticipate in your presentation. Don't be embarrassed or humiliated if you occasionally find yourself stuck for an answer—after all, you're discussing the sum total of *208 million* people's life activities, making lapses in knowledge a given.

Once you've warmed up the first tentative audience of family and close friends, get them to read this book themselves, so that they can join you in your private campaign for a better life while you yourself advance to level number 2 and *start talking with your coworkers.*

There's so much going on in the world these days that it's virtually impossible to communicate anything more than a fraction of total available information to anything more than a fraction of the total population. It takes a tremendous effort and a mountain of dollars to communicate effectively via the mass media. Of the mass media, books are probably the least far reaching. Individual titles, even the most eagerly bought and read best sellers, achieve very low levels of mass-audience coverage. For instance, *The Godfather,* an enormous commercial success, has only reached approximately 10 percent of total U.S. households. In other words, you cannot presume that people will have read what you have read, and know what you know, even if the subject may be of great interest to them.

Instead, take the knowledge to them yourself. Make your co-workers and business acquaintances *aware* of this new system by *telling* them about it.

Having done so, you and they will be in a position to do something constructive about it *where it counts,* namely at the grass roots within your company. Although there seem to be many profit-motivated benefits inherent in the 8-Day Week, benefits which should spark management's interest, it is unrealistic to assume that members of management will have come in full contact with the concept—much less heard of it at all. It is up to you to bring it to their attention in a coherent, thoughtful manner. Only you and your fellow workers can accurately determine the 8-Day Week's relevance to your own company.

If you're involved with a small company, it won't be so difficult for you and your colleagues to cover the ground necessary to form an intelligent, informed argument for presentation to management.

If you're a little cog in a big machine, it will be far more complicated. In this case, it would seem sensible to muster as many arguments as possible from people involved in operations and departments which differ from your own immediate area of activity.

If you belong to a union whose members work for more than one company, you're *really* in the driver's seat. All you have to do is spread the word, form study and recommendation committees, come up with an intelligent, affordable set of designs for conversion applicable to the various companies concerned . . . and go have a chat with them.

Whether you are in a union situation or not, it is of the utmost importance that your proposals and rationales be solidly based and thoroughly considered before they are presented to management. Poor preparation can lead to lack of sympathy toward a recommendation; its rejection; erection of barriers between employers and employees; a general worsening in relations between the two.

At the same time that you work to encourage study and adoption of the 8-Day Week by your employer, you might make the effort to enlist your wife or husband, whether employed or otherwise, in the work of passing the word. Most particularly, however, you should involve your children.

Young people tend to be fairly sophisticated these days, as well as open-minded, vocal, and enthusiastic. Involving them can rapidly accelerate the process of generating broad awareness of the concept and widespread discussion of it.

Furthermore, young people are a pipeline to *teachers,* who are a unique and valuable communications medium in themselves. They not only communicate with your children in their own classroom encounters, as well as with many other young people in other classes during the course of a teaching week, but also with fellow teachers, many parents, friends, and neighbors.

Your kids, then, can form the first flakes in what can quickly become a communications snowstorm.

An element in public life which is fairly responsive to public sentiment and the needs of the people is politicians. Although it may be assumed that certain elected officials will remain remote and unresponsive to any efforts to gain their attention, there seems to be an increasing trend among them to listen to and consider communications from their constituents. Such representatives of the people should be sympathetic to a concept which offers economic and other advantages nationwide, as well as the promise of a better life to the voters they represent. Letters to such people would, therefore, seem appropriate.

Perhaps a final word on the subject of this country as the logical birthplace for the 8-Day Week would be in order. Despite its short history, the United States has carried an immense load of leadership to the world at large—leadership in social and political concepts, leadership in scientific theory and technique, leadership in economic thought and application. Despite the continued presence of our natural and man-made assets, and an enormously gifted population, something has gone wrong. There seems to be a general lack of vitality among the people, accompanied by an ebbing sense of leadership as well as the ability to lead the world in its reach for a spectrum of humanistic and practical goals.

I feel that this leadership should be resumed not in the blindly chauvinistic belief that "the U.S. is best" but rather because such leadership, which can benefit billions of non-Americans worldwide, will not be forthcoming from any other country.

The meaning of this peroration, and in a greater sense this whole book, is put far more skillfully by Robert Frost in two stanzas from his poem "America Is Hard to See":

> Had but Columbus known enough
> He might have boldly made the bluff
> That better than da Gama's gold
> He had been given to behold
> The race's future trial place,
> A fresh start for the human race.
>
> .   .   .   .
>
> But all he did was spread the room
> Of our enacting out the doom
> Of being in each other's way,
> And so put off the weary day
> When we would have to put our mind
> On how to crowd but still be kind.

Notes

1: A Brief Survey of Our Urban Ills

page

1   Since over two-thirds: U.S. Bureau of the Census, *Statistical Abstract of the United States: 1970*, 91st edition (Washington, D.C.: Government Printing Office, 1970).

1   "about a man who is beset by urban despairs": *New York Times*, Nov. 15, 1971, p. 54.

2   "the urban headache": Diane Zimmerman, "The Urban Headache: Is There Fast Fast Fast Relief," *New York*, Oct. 25, 1971, pp. 40–44.

2   "The international Road Federation . . .": *Wall Street Journal*, Nov. 8, 1971, p. 32.

3   Robert N. Rickles: *New York Times*, Dec. 31, 1971, p. 1.

4   New York's progress toward that goal: *New York Times*, Jan. 17, 1972, p. 29.

4   The Environmental Protection Agency: "Mounting Pressure to Curb Downtown Driving," *U.S. News & World Report*, March 13, 1972, pp. 74–77.

5   mass-transit labor costs: "Attacking the Mass Transit Mess," *Business Week*, June 3, 1972, pp. 60–65.

5   output per man-hour declined: U.S. Bureau of Labor Statistics, *Indexes of Output per Man-Hour Selected Industries 1939 and 1947–70* (Bulletin 1692) (Washington, D.C.: Government Printing Office, 1971).

5   ". . . a mere .1% increase . . .": "The Limits of Productivity," *Time*, November 15, 1971, p. 24.

6-7   *graphs*: U.S. Bureau of Labor Statistics, *Handbook of Labor Statistics* (Washington, D.C.: Government Printing Office, 1971).

8   between 1950 and 1970: U.S. Bureau of Labor Statistics, *Em-

page

ployment & Earnings for the United States 1909–1970 (Bulletin 1312–7) (Washington, D.C.: Government Printing Office, 1971).

9   Since then, the situation has deteriorated: "Is the Shift to Services Really a Drag?" *Business Week*, Sept. 9, 1972, p. 85.

9   disagreement with official statistics: *New York Post*, November 11, 1971, p. 57.

2: We're Getting Less For More

11   suburban populations have increased: "Mounting Pressure to Curb Downtown Driving," *U.S. News & World Report*, March 13, 1972, pp. 74–77.

13   James Beggs: "Attacking the Mass Transit Mess," *Business Week*, June 3, 1972, pp. 60–65.

13   The federal government estimates: ibid.

13   At least twelve U.S. cities: ibid.

14   " 'The problem,' one Transportation Department official said: *New York Times*, Jan. 30, 1972, p. 50.

14   Volpe: "Attacking the Mass Transit Mess."

15   "The Public Service Commission . . .": *New York Times*, Jan. 18, 1972, p. 1.

15   Ma Bell: "A Present for Ma Bell," *Time*, Dec. 4, 1972, p. 45.

16   sewage disposal plant: *New York Times*, Oct. 21, 1971, p. 59.

18   Yearly state and local tax: *New York Times*, Jan. 31, 1972, p. 1.

3: Getting The Job Done

23   In 1970, for example: U.S. Bureau of Labor Statistics, *Employment & Earnings for the United States 1909–1970* (Bulletin 1312–7) (Washington, D.C.: Government Printing Office, 1971).

25   Their workweek lengthened: ibid.

34   "What the company is discovering . . .": *New York Times*, Feb. 3, 1972, p. 38.

37   "Mayor Lindsay said yesterday . . .": *New York Times*, October 20, 1971, p. 20.

40   "At the rate . . .": Alvin Toffler, *Future Shock* (New York: Random House, 1970).

42   "The accelerative thrust . . .": ibid.

page

91st edition (Washington, D.C.: Government Printing Office, 1970).

103   state legislation: Eileen Hoffman, "The Four-Day Week Raises New Problems," *The Conference Board Record*, February 1972.

104   "The solution may be . . .": "Where Have All the Jobs Gone?" *Forbes*, Aug. 1, 1972, pp. 17–23.

9: Alternatives to the 8-Day Week

106   The 4-day week: Riva Poor, *4 Days, 40 Hours* (Cambridge, Mass.: Bursk & Poor, 1970), passim.

107   The firms surveyed: ibid.

109   an American Management Association national survey: *Los Angeles Times*, April 9, 1972, Section G, p. 2.

110   one company's experience with the 4-day week: Thomas Vris, "New Work Week Schedules—Some Implications for Management," presented at the University of Pittsburgh, Graduate School of Business, Pittsburgh, Nov. 4, 1971.

113   Another company: *New York Times*, April 6, 1972, p. 45.

10: 8-Day Economics

116   "Five years of inflation . . .": "Productivity Our Biggest Undeveloped Resource," *Business Week,* Sept. 9, 1972, pp. 79–150.

117   Edward Denison: "Lower Productivity Threatens Growth," *Business Week*, Jan. 1, 1972, pp. 35–37.

118   Between 1969 and 1971: *New York Post*, March 7, 1972, p. 65.

118   A survey of several hundred: "The Job Gap for College Graduates in the '70s," *Business Week*, Sept. 23, 1972, pp. 48–58.

119   The year 1971: "Balance of Payments—And $31 Billion Down," *Time*, Jan. 31, 1972, p. 17.

120   "During the 1970's . . .": *Wall Street Journal*, Feb. 9, 1972, p. 1.

120   Between 1960 and 1970: "Empty Pockets on a Trillion Dollars a Year," *Time*, March 13, 1972, pp. 66–74.

121   In 1971, citizens voted down: ibid.

121   New York State appears: *New York Times*, April 2, 1972, p. 1.

121   New York City can't make ends meet: "Empty Pockets on a Trillion Dollars a Year."

page
122 employing approximately 19 percent: "Productivity Our Biggest Undeveloped Resource."
123 The interstate highway system: "Empty Pockets on a Trillion Dollars a Year."
123 It costs approximately $5 million: "Attacking the Mass Transit Mess," *Business Week*, June 3, 1972, pp. 60–65.
124 *Business Week* states: "The Job Gap for College Graduates in the '70s."
126 "Yet the hard fact . . .": "Productivity Our Biggest Undeveloped Resource."
127 William W. Bewley, Jr.: ibid.
127 In a plant situation: ibid.
131 It has been estimated: ibid.
132 Since road vehicles: "Attacking the Mass Transit Mess."
133 Between 1972 and 1977: *New York Times*, Jan. 30, 1972, p. 23.

11: Making It Happen

135 "I needed a work schedule . . .": Riva Poor, *40 Days, 40 Hours* (Cambridge, Mass.: Bursk & Poor, 1970), pp. 169–70.

For Further Reading

"The High Price of More Electric Power." *Business Week*, Aug. 19, 1972, pp. 54–58.

"Learning to Live with Phase II." *Time*, Nov. 29, 1971, p. 31.

Poor, Riva. *4 Days, 40 Hours*. Cambridge, Mass.: Bursk & Poor, 1970.

"Pressure on Ford to Test a Shorter Work Week." *Business Week*, May 27, 1972, p. 50.

"The Raging Fight Over Burke-Hartke." *Business Week*, Feb. 12, 1972, pp. 14–16.

Toffler, Alvin. *Future Shock*. New York: Random House, 1970.

"Why Joblessness May Stay High." *Business Week*, April 15, 1972, p. 44.

"The Worst Is Yet to Be?" *Time*, Jan. 24, 1972, p. 32.

Index

153